AMAZING ACTS
—act one

Acts 1:1 to 9:31

Enjoy the real life drama of ACTS

by Gerard Chrispin

EP BOOKS

1st Floor Venture House, 6 Silver Court, Watchmead,
Welwyn Garden City, UK, AL7 1TS

web: www.epbooks.org

e-mail: sales@epbooks.org

EP books are distributed in the USA by:
JPL Fulfillment
3741 Linden Avenue Southeast,
Grand Rapids, MI 49548
orders@jplfulfillment.com
Tel: 877.683.6935

© Gerard Chrispin 2015. All rights reserved. No part of this publication may be reproduced, stored in a retrieval system or transmitted, in any form, or by any means, electronic, mechanical, photocopying, recording or otherwise, without the prior permission of the publishers.

First published in 2015

British Library Cataloguing in Publication Data available
ISBN: 978–1–78397–080–3

All Scripture quotations, unless otherwise indicated, are taken from the New King James Version. Copyright © 1979, 1980, 1982 by Thomas Nelson, Inc. Used by permission. All rights reserved.

Printed by Bell and Bain Ltd, Glasgow.

This book is dedicated to Bible-believing churches and Christians worldwide who suffer because their 'crimes' are to believe in the Lord Jesus Christ, uphold the Bible as God's word, and to share its good news with others. Jesus alone is *the way, the truth and the life* (John 14:6). They know they *ought to obey God rather than men* (Acts 5:29) even if that costs them their freedom and their lives.

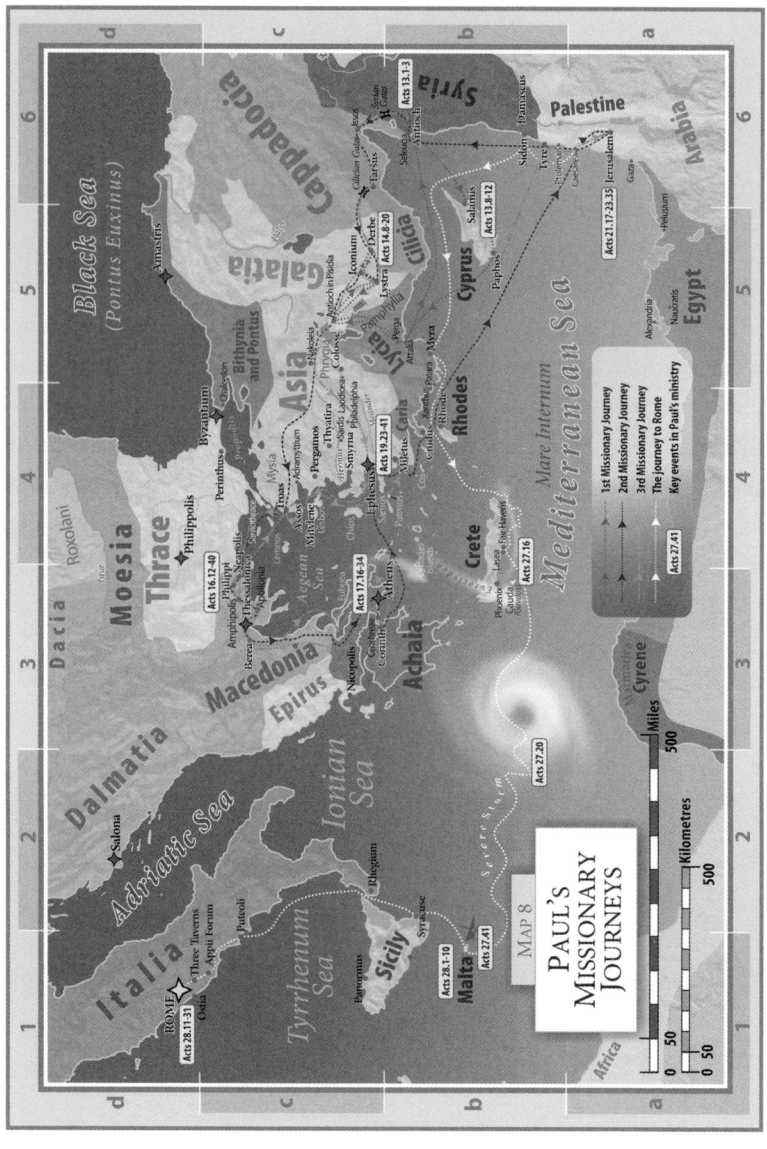

Contents

	Amazing Acts—act one in Audio	7
	Foreword by Chris	9
	A word from the author	11
	*Amazing Acts—*Overview	15
	Enjoy the real life drama of Acts	19
1	An explosive start!—Acts 1:1–14	21
2	Peter restored, Judas ruined, and a decision reached —Acts 1:15–26	27
3	The Day of Pentecost—Acts 2:1–13	33
4	What a message!—Acts 2:14–36	39
5	What a response!—Acts 2:37–41	47
6	Our first glimpse of the early church—Acts 2:42–47	53
7	A brand new walk—Acts 3:1–10	59
8	Peter preaches again—Acts 3:11–26	65
9	In custody and in court—Acts 4:1–12	71
10	Prejudice, priority, prayer and practice—Acts 4:13–37	77
11	A double death—Acts 5:1–11	85
12	In prison again! and out again!—Acts 5:12–32	91
13	Enter Gamaliel—Acts 5:33–42	97

14 A problem solved, the word spread, and opposition stirred—Acts 6:1–15	103
15 Stephen's defence before the Council—Acts 7:1–53	111
16 Faithfulness, martyrdom and Saul of Tarsus—Acts 7:54–60	121
17 'The blood of the martyrs is the seed of the Church'—Acts 8:1–8	127
18 Sorcery—Acts 8:9–25	133
19 A truly amazing conversion—Acts 8:26–40	141
20 The Damascus Road experience—and beyond—Acts 9:1–20	149
21 Not so easy for Saul—Acts 9:20–31	157
A final word	165
How to run *Amazing Acts—Act One* discussion groups	169
Amazing Acts—act one correspondence courses	177
Endnotes	

Listen, chapter by chapter, to the Amazing Acts trilogy (Amazing Acts—act one, Amazing Acts—act two, and Amazing Acts—act three) at amazingacts.net

The whole text is also printed there to read. Download free of charge the complete audio of the Amazing Acts trilogy from that web site, including 'ISO' files to create your own audio CDs.

Ready made CDs are also available from the publisher. Ask for details

Foreword by Chris

I first attended a *Mark Time*[1] Discussion Group whilst on remand in prison, unsure of the Christian faith. I had no prior knowledge of the Bible. I was a lost and hurting soul looking for meaning in life. Sitting in that group with the other offenders, I felt different. I was touched by the peace in the room and the love and joy that emanated from the leaders. They seemed to have what I craved for—meaning in their lives.

As the Word of God was played on the CD player and as the chapters and verses were discussed amongst the group and explained by the leader I began to realise that only by having a relationship with Jesus Christ would I ever be able to obtain that same peace, joy and meaning to my life. I returned to my cell that day with a thirst for knowledge and a hunger to read more of the Bible. I spent the time in my cell reading *Mark Time* over and over and I could not get enough of it as the words were speaking directly into my life. I attended a few more sessions and one day I gave my life to Jesus Christ in my cell. Thanks to the Biblical truths clearly and simply explained by the leader I was able to have a secure a foundation of Scripture to stand upon and I have learned so much in such a short space of time about my Lord and Saviour through *Mark Time*.

After a while I was moved to another prison so I could no longer attend the *Mark Time* Discussion Group but I am so thankful that I was able to bring the Correspondence Course with me. Everywhere I go now I can read a portion of Mark's Gospel and have it clearly explained to me by the excellent exposition of the Word in bite-sized chapters. *Mark Time* has been such a valuable tool for me in helping me to grow as a Christian and it is the first book I recommend after the Bible when I share my faith with someone. I recommend the book to all and I promise that you will be blessed to read it. I still am.

I am honoured to be asked to write a reference. I have never written a reference before so I have just spoken or written from the heart. Regarding *Amazing Acts* I pray that God will use it to bless many just as *Mark Time* has.

'Chris'[2]
(Full correct name, ID and location supplied)

A word from the author

I remember the thrill of experiencing God's speaking to me in my early twenties through the Saturday night Bible study run by Leeds Young Life. I had been backsliding and my Saturday nights had been spent in very different ways than studying the Bible, especially after playing rugby each Saturday afternoon. That Bible study was on the Acts of the Apostles, and I have never forgotten how, week after week, I learned more and more of God's grace to me and of my duty to love and serve my Lord and Saviour wholeheartedly.

If reading or studying this book or listening to it being read can help to lead others to Christ, or to come back to Him and also serve Him wholeheartedly, I shall be thrilled again! God's hand of blessing has been on *Mark Time* and its associated optional Discussion Course and Correspondence Course. I have followed a similar pattern in writing this book though there is no separate book to explain the Discussion Groups. Instead I have done this in Appendix Two of this book. I have also provided in Appendix One some helpful details about the separate Correspondence Course for any who wish to use it.

The same wonderfully supportive team that helped to get *Mark Time* off the ground has again helped with *Amazing Acts—act one,* and I very much hope and pray that, God willing, they will do so again for *Amazing Acts—act two* (Acts 9:32 to 18:23) and *Amazing Acts—act three* (Acts 18:24 to 28:31), both to follow soon. So thank you again to David Harding (*Milnrow Evangelical Church, United Beach Missions,* and *The Christian Answer*), Derek French (retired from *Grace Baptist Mission,* but still working hard for Christ at home and abroad), and my wife, best friend and helper, Phillippa. David has helped by suggesting changes to the original manuscript, helping to format it, and has made sure that *Amazing Acts,* under the title *amazingacts.net* will be read and listened to on the world wide web, whether by desktop computers, laptops, or any other appliance that can get online. Derek is solely responsible for recording the CDs. Phillippa has helped me right through the writing process, from start to finish. I am also grateful to her for recording the Bible readings as she did for *Mark Time.* Thank you too to David Fortune (*Christian Prison Resources Ministries*) for his most helpful inputs, particularly about the Correspondence Course.

I am grateful to 'Chris' (not his real name) for the very kind foreword, which he provided with no prompting from me or anyone else. He has trusted Christ in a UK prison and such is the change that family members and inmates have come to Christ too. I hope that God will bless you or anyone to whom you give or recommend this book– whether an individual or a group—in the way that Chris has been blessed through its companion, *Mark Time.* 'Salvation is of the Lord' (Jonah 2:9). My hope is that churches, fellowships, groups, missions and prisons will be blessed through studying this amazing book of Acts and that many will put their trust in the Lord Jesus and follow Him in discipleship.

At a time when the clouds of opposition to the Christian gospel seem to thicken threateningly in the west, may the message of Acts help more and more people to sort out the things that matter most. We preach the crucified, risen, ascended and coming Lord Jesus Christ knowing that *there is no 'salvation in any other, for there is no other name under heaven given among men by which we must be saved'* (Acts 4:12). If and when urged to deny or dilute His message of saving grace we must refuse. *We ought to obey God rather than men.*

Gerard Chrispin

Amazing Acts—Overview

The 28 chapters of the Acts of the Apostles are covered in three books, *Amazing Acts—act one*, *Amazing Acts—act two*, and *Amazing Acts—act three*.

This Overview shows how the three parts relate to each other in dividing up the Acts of the Apostle.

Amazing Acts—act one (Acts 1:1–9:31) covers the birth, growth, witness and cruel persecution of the church up to the conversion and early evangelistic ministry of Saul, later to be known as Paul.

- Jesus' commission to the church to witness to Him *in Jerusalem, and in all Judea and Samaria, and to the end of the earth* (Acts 1:8).
- The birth, growth, witness, and persecution of the church in Jerusalem (Acts 1:1 to Acts 8:3).
- The spread of the gospel into Judea and Samaria by Christians fleeing persecution (Acts 8:4).
- Concentration of gospel preaching in Samaria by Philip, Peter and John (Acts 8:4–25).
- Concentration of gospel preaching in Judea by Philip (Acts 8:26–40).

- Moving on from Jerusalem, Judea and Samaria: the conversion and nurturing of Saul, the arch-persecutor of the church, near Damascus in Syria (Acts 9:1–19); Saul immediately preaches the gospel in Damascus with the believers there (Acts 9:20–22); After a Jewish death-threat Saul flees to Jerusalem via Caesarea (Judea), from where he escapes another death-threat by going north to his home town of Tarsus in Cilicia. (Acts 9:23–30).
- A period of freedom from persecution and further growth for the church, after Saul's departure (Acts 9:31).

Amazing Acts—act two (Acts 9:32–18:23) covers Peter's gospel preaching in Judea, the wider spread of the gospel, persecution through Herod, Paul's first two missionary trips which take the gospel wider still toward *the end of the earth*; between those missionary trips Saul attends the meeting of the apostle's Council:

- Peter's evangelistic ministry in Judea at Lydda, in the plain of Sharon, and at Joppa (Acts 9:32–43).
- Peter's witness in Caesarea (Judea) to the Gentile, Cornelius; the falling of the Holy Spirit on the believing Gentiles; after Peter's debriefing is discussed, the rejoicing of the apostles and believers that Gentiles are converted (Acts 10:1–11:18).
- The spread of the gospel further to Phoenicia, Cyprus, and Antioch; Barnabas brings Saul from Tarsus to Antioch; famine relief arranged for Judean Christians through Barnabas and Saul. (Acts 11:19–30).
- Herod Agrippa's persecution of the church and martyrdom of some leaders; Peter in and out of prison; Growth of God's word; return of Barnabas and Saul from Jerusalem (Acts 12:1–25).
- Paul's first missionary trip (Acts 13:1–14:28).

- The Council of apostles and elders at Jerusalem about salvation by faith alone (Acts 15:1–35).
- Paul's second missionary trip (Acts 15:36–18:23).

Amazing Acts—act three (Acts 18:24–28:31) covers the last of Paul's three missionary ventures, Paul in Jerusalem again, his hearings before various authorities leading to his going to Rome to appeal his case to Caesar, his arrival there and freedom to share God's word for two years:

- Paul's third missionary trip (Acts 18:24–21:16).
- Paul in Jerusalem with the apostles and elders; his arrest in the temple; facing, speaking and testifying to a mob from which he is rescued by the soldiers (Acts 21:17–22:29);
- Paul's appearances before the Council (Sanhedrin) in Jerusalem and Felix in Caesarea, and Festus through whom he appeals to Caesar; further appearance before King Agrippa and his testimony to the king (Acts 22:30–26:32);
- Paul's very eventful journey to Rome via a shipwreck on Malta; his ministry there to Jewish leaders, and his relative freedom to preach about Jesus Christ for two years 'no-one forbidding him' (Acts 27:1–28:31).

INTRODUCTION

Enjoy the real life drama of Acts

Welcome to *Amazing Acts—act one*! What could be more exciting, challenging or relevant today than to see how a small, dejected and defeated body of believers became the first members of the early church which, though sorely persecuted, were empowered by the Holy Spirit to turn the world upside down with the gospel?

Each chapter of *Amazing Acts—act one* whether in writing or by audio, contains the passage of the book of Acts covered in that chapter. *Amazing Acts—act one* covers the first nine chapters of Acts, except for a few verses which best fit into *Amazing Acts—act two*.

How can you best use this book for your own and for others' blessing? (The Correspondence Course book and Appendix One to this book explain how best to use that course.)

1. Pray that God will help you understand and trust His word, and put it into practice in your life.
2. Play the relevant track and listen to the passage and explanation while you read it in the book.
3. Read two or three times through the verses of Acts printed in each chapter of *Amazing Acts—act one*.
4. Ask 'What is the main point of the passage?' How do the footnoted Bible references relate to that?
5. Answer the three questions in each chapter, using the Bible verses noted there to help you.
6. Pray over what you have learned. Ask God to help you to apply it faithfully to your own life.
7. Read and listen through the chapter again to see if you have missed anything important.

You may adapt these points to use *Amazing Acts—act one* for Bible studies, study groups, or one-on-one teaching.

Amazing Acts—act one may be used with any Bible translation of the book of Acts, although the New King James Version ('NKJV') is the one generally quoted. The Bible references function as follows: Acts 1:1–14 means Acts chapter 1, verses 1 to 14.

CHAPTER 1

An explosive start!

ACTS 1:1–14

1 *The former account I made, O Theophilus, of all that Jesus began both to do and teach,* 2 *until the day in which He was taken up, after He through the Holy Spirit had given commandments to the apostles whom He had chosen,* 3 *to whom He also presented Himself alive after His suffering by many infallible proofs, being seen by them during forty days and speaking of the things pertaining to the kingdom of God.* 4 *And being assembled together with them, He commanded them not to depart from Jerusalem, but to wait for the Promise of the Father, 'which,' He said, 'you have heard from Me;* 5 *for John truly baptized with water, but you shall be baptized with the Holy Spirit not many days from now.'* 6 *Therefore, when they had come together, they asked Him, saying, 'Lord, will You at this time restore the kingdom to Israel?'* 7 *And He said to them, 'It is not for you to know times or seasons which the Father has put in His own authority.* 8 *But you shall receive power when the Holy Spirit has come upon you; and you*

shall be witnesses to Me in Jerusalem, and in all Judea and Samaria, and to the end of the earth.' 9 *Now when He had spoken these things, while they watched, He was taken up, and a cloud received Him out of their sight.* 10 *And while they looked steadfastly toward heaven as He went up, behold, two men stood by them in white apparel,* 11 *who also said, 'Men of Galilee, why do you stand gazing up into heaven? This same Jesus, who was taken up from you into heaven, will so come in like manner as you saw Him go into heaven.'* 12 *Then they returned to Jerusalem from the mount called Olivet, which is near Jerusalem, a Sabbath day's journey.* 13 *And when they had entered, they went up into the upper room where they were staying: Peter, James, John, and Andrew; Philip and Thomas; Bartholomew and Matthew; James the son of Alphaeus and Simon the Zealot; and Judas the son of James.* 14 *These all continued with one accord in prayer and supplication, with the women and Mary the mother of Jesus, and with His brothers.*

Acts 1:1–3
The facts about Acts—and an explosive start

Theophilus has a lot of reading to do! But he is used to it. Luke has already addressed his gospel to him.[1] In it he shared established facts about Jesus' birth, life, teaching, miracles, death on the cross for our sins and rising again. Now Luke leads us to the thrilling start, growth and early adventures of Christ's new church. Like footprints in newly fallen snow, we will follow the tracks of the early Christians.

Acts 1:10–11 takes over where Luke 24 finished, with Christ's ascension to Heaven. What an explosive start to a new era! Before that, the risen Jesus had often met with and taught His disciples. That provided some of the 'many infallible proofs' that after His death on the cross He rose from the tomb. The risen Lord appeared to many people in different circumstances and at different times.[2] Credible, first-hand, and consistent eye-witnesses testified to this. Such strong evidence would gladden the heart of any courtroom advocate! This gripping book of Acts is no fairy tale. Like the rest of God's word, the Bible, it is God-breathed[3] and entirely trustworthy. As you read it, you can trust it!

Acts 1:4–8
A staggering mission statement—and how to achieve it

Jesus was fully Man and fully God. At one meal with His disciples He told them that one day, as they waited at Jerusalem, God would keep His promise of baptizing them with the Holy Spirit.[4] John the Baptist had immersed willing converts to Christ into water to signal their turning from wrong in their lives.[5] Jesus would place under the life-changing power of the Holy Spirit anyone who turned to Him from sin. The Bible teaches that when the Holy Spirit comes to live within each new believer in Christ He also places that new Christian into the body of Christ, namely His worldwide church.[6] The Holy Spirit's first task is to convict us of our sinfulness and unrighteous lives, for which we deserve God's eternal judgement.[7] He then points us to Jesus who bore our sins and our deserved judgement when He died on the cross in our place.[8]

The Holy Spirit changes the lives and eternal destiny of those who receive Christ. He also helps weak Christians to fulfil Jesus' demanding mission statement of Acts 1:8, to share His good news 'in Jerusalem, and in all Judea (which surrounds Jerusalem) and Samaria, and to the end of the earth'. We must continue to make Christ known 'here, there and everywhere' by our changed lives and language. Great blessing awaits those who trust in Jesus as they tell others about their Saviour.

Acts 1:9–11
He is going! He is coming again!
The last words of loved ones and famous people are often remembered. Listen to those last words of our risen Saviour before He ascends miraculously to His heavenly home. Jesus is far more than a religious teacher. Everything He is and all He has said and done reach their climax in His ascension to Heaven. No mere man could ever do that! Man on the moon caused great wonder and acclaim. God's coming from Heaven to earth in human flesh and then returning, make mere moon landings look trivial by comparison. And He came to save sinners. That too is special.

Jesus will return in glory.[9] The New Testament is full of that certain hope. He will come to judge those who do not turn from sin and trust Him. He will take back with Him those who know Him as their Saviour and Lord.[10] Jesus, as judge, will seal each person's eternal destiny

Acts 1:12–14
But life must go on. The power house for weaklings!
After witnessing Jesus' ascension His disciples now return home from the Mount of Olives. Previously they cowered away in fear and 'froze' after Jesus's crucifixion, like rabbits caught in car headlights. They were not easily convinced about the resurrection, but were later persuaded by the facts. Now God gives them great confidence in Him. They return to the upper room to pray. In future, personal individual confidence in Christ and the encouragement brought by praying together will help them live for their Saviour in an often-hostile world. Others join in to pray with the eleven remaining leaders.[11] Humble women who have served Jesus faithfully accompany His own mother

and His formerly sceptical and critical brothers.[12] They pray with the apostles. Joining in prayer together with others in a prayer meeting becomes a new blessing when Christ becomes your Lord and Saviour. But they now have a difficult choice to make, as we shall see soon.

Questions on Chapter 1
An Explosive Start!—Acts 1:1–14

A. What confidence can you have that you can really trust that the account in the book of Acts is true?
Acts 1:1–3, Luke 1:3, 2 Timothy 3:14–16, 2 Peter 1:19–21

B. Why can it often be so hard to fulfil Jesus' mission statement of Acts 1:8? How does God make it possible for a new Christian to achieve it?
Acts 1:5, Acts 1:8, Matthew 28:18–20

C. What does Acts 1:1–11 teach about Jesus? What do you learn about prayer in Acts 1:12–14? Is there a connection between them?
Acts 1:1–11, Acts 1:12–14, Philippians 4:6–7, Revelation 1:17–18, Hebrews 7:25

CHAPTER 2

Peter restored, Judas ruined, and a decision reached

ACTS 1:15–26

15 And in those days Peter stood up in the midst of the disciples (altogether the number of names was about a hundred and twenty), and said, 16 'Men and brethren, this Scripture had to be fulfilled, which the Holy Spirit spoke before by the mouth of David concerning Judas, who became a guide to those who arrested Jesus; 17 for he was numbered with us and obtained a part in this ministry.'

18 (Now this man purchased a field with the wages of iniquity; and falling headlong, he burst open in the middle and all his entrails gushed out. 19 And it became known to all those dwelling in Jerusalem; so that field is called in their own language, Akel Dama, that is, Field of Blood.)

20 'For it is written in the Book of Psalms:

'Let his dwelling place be desolate,
And let no one live in it';

and,

'Let another take his office.'

[21] 'Therefore, of these men who have accompanied us all the time that the Lord Jesus went in and out among us, [22] beginning from the baptism of John to that day when He was taken up from us, one of these must become a witness with us of His resurrection.'

[23] And they proposed two: Joseph called Barsabas, who was surnamed Justus, and Matthias. [24] And they prayed and said, 'You, O Lord, who know the hearts of all, show which of these two You have chosen [25] to take part in this ministry and apostleship from which Judas by transgression fell, that he might go to his own place.' [26] And they cast their lots, and the lot fell on Matthias. And he was numbered with the eleven apostles.

Acts 1:15–17
From denials to decision—Peter's progress

Mark's last recorded comment on Peter is that he broke down and wept.[1] Earlier, Peter rashly promised Jesus never to desert Him. Jesus warned him that he would deny Him three times before the rooster crowed twice. Yet Peter boasted, 'If I have to die with You, I will not deny You'.[2] His triple denial followed.[3] Facing cruel and unjust treatment on His way to die on the cross, Jesus 'turned and looked at Peter'.[4] Peter was broken.

Later, he inspected Jesus' empty tomb, and met His risen Lord.[5] He then spent time with Jesus and saw Him ascend to Heaven.[6]

Much in the first part of the book of Acts shows how God the Holy Spirit transforms and strengthens Peter.[7]

We too can stray from God. But He always offers a way back. Peter himself reminds us that Jesus died to 'bring us to God'.[8] He forgives, cleanses from sin, and indwells by His Spirit all who confess and forsake sin, and trust Christ alone. He saves us from sin's penalty and power.

Peter, now restored and an apostle,[9] begins to show real leadership qualities. He tells about a hundred and twenty Christians what the Holy Spirit predicted about Judas in God's word, through King David.[10] God blesses repentant failures like Peter and uses them in His service. That comforts every Christian! Peter now deals with the leadership gap caused by Judas' suicide after betraying Jesus.

Acts 1:18–19
How and why did Judas die?

On that dark betrayal night Judas had identified God's Son to the bloodthirsty, arresting mob, by greeting Him with a kiss.[11] The mob was manipulated by cynical Jewish religious leaders and took Jesus by night because the ordinary people would have stopped them in daylight. Then Jesus was insulted, abused, blasphemed, beaten, unjustly tried, wrongly convicted, flogged and crucified.[12] The Jewish leaders had paid Judas—the apostles' treasurer and a thief—thirty silver pieces to betray Christ. Full of remorse because of his sad and lost condition, but never truly repentant for his sins,[13] the sad traitor returned his money. Refusing to accept back this *blood money*, the religious leaders bought a field with it, calling it 'Field of Blood'.[14] Guilt ridden, Judas hanged himself. And 'falling headlong' his intestines burst open.[15] Perhaps his corpse fell from a tree where he hanged himself onto rocks below? Or maybe his body was ripped open by hitting a tree branch in his rapid descent? The death of the unrepentant betrayer, 'doomed to destruction',[16] fulfilled Scripture. Compare the blessing of Peter's restoration with the misery of Judas' suicide and eternal judgement. Real repentance and personal faith in Christ always precede forgiveness and restoration.[17]

Acts 1:20–22
Finding a replacement

Peter quotes David from the Psalms,[18] and urges his colleagues to choose an apostle to fill the gap left by Judas.[19] The arch-persecutor of Christians, Saul, will soon be converted to Christ and later become the apostle Paul: but the apostles can now predict neither Saul's conversion nor God's choosing him as the apostle to succeed Judas.[20]

'Apostle' means 'sent one'. In a general sense each Christian is a 'sent one', sent by God to help and bless others and share Jesus Christ's good news with them. But the Bible reveals twelve historic apostles (thirteen, after Paul is added to Matthias). 'Historic', means each apostle is a one-off, foundational apostle with a unique once-for-all God-given task. The New Testament was written through the authority and influence God gave them. Faultlessly inspired by the Holy Spirit the New Testament was added to the Old Testament to complete the Bible as God's written word.[21]

Peter now gives three qualifications of God's historic apostles. First, they accompanied the other apostles throughout Jesus' time with them on earth. That started when John the Baptist prepared the way for Jesus by baptising people who saw their need to repent. Second, they had met Jesus after His resurrection as the risen Lord. Third, they witnessed Christ's ascension into

Heaven. God marks out these apostles—and some of their close associates—by enabling them to perform specific miraculous signs and wonders. These show the apostles are God's chosen team through whom He reveals His word and His gospel in the New Testament. Paul says these signs are 'the signs of an apostle—signs, and wonders and mighty deeds'. God is saying, 'These men teach my unique message. Listen to them!'

Acts 1:23–26
Guidance, unity and how to make a difficult decision together

The eleven apostles now work together in their decision-making. These like-minded believers are fully committed to Christ personally, believe the Bible, pray together, and value each other's fellowship. Yet they may validly have differing views on who should succeed Judas, or even if now is the time to choose a successor.

They commit all this in prayer to God, trusting Him for His answer. This cements their unity together. Unable to choose whether Barsabas or Matthias is the successful candidate, they draw lots to decide.[22] Drawing lots is an impartial way to reach a difficult decision, rather like throwing a dice. Matthias is chosen. No unpleasant disunity follows. They all regard the decision as God's.[23]

When God is put first, difficult joint decisions can be reached despite differences of opinion. Christian oneness depends on each individual believer trusting and following Jesus closely through His word under the Holy Spirit's influence. 1 John 1:7 assures Christians that if together 'we walk in the light, as He [God] is in the light, we have fellowship with one another, and the blood of Jesus, His Son, cleanses us from all sin'. Here the apostles together identify the issues clearly, pray together about them, think objectively, trust God to guide and overrule, and stand united behind their decision.

You, too, can know God's guidance in your life and make right choices if you stay close to the Guide, the Lord Jesus,[24] and follow the teaching of His word, the Bible.

Questions on Chapter 2
Peter restored, Judas ruined, and a decision reached—Acts 1:15–26

A. Trace Peter's downfall and restoration before he starts serving Christ in Acts 1:15, by using the verses quoted below. What causes his restoration?
Acts 1:15–22, Mark 14:66–72, 14:27–31, Luke 22:60–62, Luke 24:12, 33–36, John 20:19–20, 26, John 1:1–23, Acts 1:9–11, Luke 24:50–53, Mark 16:19

B. What lessons and warnings are there in this passage as you consider Judas? Compare Judas with Peter.
Acts 1:15–20, Matthew 26:47–56, John 18:1–14, Matthew 26:15, Matthew 27:3–8, John 12:4–6

C. What qualifications does Peter summarise in Acts 1:21–22 as being necessary for the apostles to bear in mind in appointing a new apostle? How would those qualifications help Judas' successor in his role as an apostle? Which of those three conditions do you think is most important and why?
Mark 1:16–20, Acts 1:10–11, 15–20, Luke 24:12, 33, 36, 50–53, John 20:19–20, 26, John 21:1–23

CHAPTER 3

The Day of Pentecost

ACTS 2:1–13

1 When the Day of Pentecost had fully come, they were all with one accord in one place. 2 And suddenly there came a sound from heaven, as of a rushing mighty wind, and it filled the whole house where they were sitting. 3 Then there appeared to them divided tongues, as of fire, and one sat upon each of them. 4 And they were all filled with the Holy Spirit and began to speak with other tongues, as the Spirit gave them utterance. 5 And there were dwelling in Jerusalem Jews, devout men, from every nation under heaven. 6 And when this sound occurred, the multitude came together, and were confused, because everyone heard them speak in his own language. 7 Then they were all amazed and marvelled, saying to one another, 'Look, are not all these who speak Galileans? 8 And how is it that we hear, each in our own language in which we were born? 9 Parthians and Medes and Elamites, those dwelling in Mesopotamia, Judea and Cappadocia, Pontus and Asia, 10 Phrygia and Pamphylia, Egypt and the parts of Libya adjoining

Cyrene, visitors from Rome, both Jews and proselytes, [11] Cretans and Arabs—we hear them speaking in our own tongues the wonderful works of God.' [12] So they were all amazed and perplexed, saying to one another, 'Whatever could this mean?' [13] Others mocking said, 'They are full of new wine'.

Acts 2:1–3
The Holy Spirit comes

Some Christians waste time arguing about secondary issues concerning the Holy Spirit. Yet there is so much important common ground to enjoy together. The apostles and over a hundred and twenty men and women now pray together in an upper room.[1] God the Holy Spirit, the third Person of the Trinity, will be their surprise Divine Guest of honour at the birth of the church on this Feast of Pentecost. He will change everything. He continues to change lives today when sinful people come to Christ for forgiveness! He makes the day that they trust Christ become their personal Pentecost.

'Pentecost' is a long established annual feast for Jewish people. It means 'fifty days', because it comes fifty days after Passover. As fifty days is essentially seven weeks it is also called the 'Feast of Weeks'. Another title, 'Feast of Harvests,' marks the Jews gathering in their harvest. They say 'Thank you' to God, by presenting to Him, as a token, the *first* part of their harvest, thus known as the 'firstfruits'.[2] So Pentecost now signals what believers in Christ *first* receive as soon as they turn to Him, namely His gift of the Holy Spirit. He comes to live in the hearts of all new believers. At the same time He makes them part of His living church.[3]

God has very special plans for *this particular* Pentecost! Those converted to Jesus on this amazing day are the firstfruits of His new-born church. Anyone, anywhere and at any time who repents and trusts in the Lord Jesus Christ becomes a living stone in that growing 'building' of people who now have come to know God.[4]

God grabs the attention of those gathered together in that upper room. A sudden sound 'as of a rushing mighty wind' fills the whole house. This huge tornado sound is from Heaven. This is God's doing. Then what seem to be 'tongues, as of fire' separate and rest on each person present. The sound is not an actual rushing wind—it just sounds like 'a rushing mighty wind'. Neither are the tongues actual tongues of fire but just seemed to be 'tongues ... of fire'.[5] Jesus had promised, 'Behold I send the Promise of my Father upon you, but tarry in the city until you are endued with power from on high'.[6] That moment has now arrived. The promised Holy Spirit has come!

Acts 2:4–12
Languages without learning

There are at least fifteen different people groups in Jerusalem to celebrate Pentecost. Many others speak different dialects and languages. God's amazing message will reach everyone and mark out this day as clear and unforgettable in world history. The world will hear that He will accept 'all men everywhere'[7] who repent from their sins, believe that His Son has died for them, and put their confidence in Him alone. The Jews, who have rejected Christ as Messiah, ought now to understand that God will save Gentiles as well as Jews.[8]

But who is sharing this message with these multi-lingual visitors? All the speakers are locals from Galilee! No language laboratories exist! No printed dictionaries are available, nor TV programmes or language teaching courses. Also, 'Galilean

Jews speak with a distinct regional accent and are regarded as unsophisticated and uneducated by some southern Judean Jews.'[9] How will God convey His message to those of different languages, especially through largely uneducated men with heavy accents and no language skills?

This is a unique experience in history.[10] As God comes to bless all His blood-bought children in that upper room by filling them with the Holy Spirit and placing them into His living church, something else happens. They begin 'to speak with other tongues, as the Spirit gave them utterance'. The word translated *tongues* means 'languages', as is obvious from what happens and what is said. In the amazed and perplexed crowd each person hears them 'speak in his own language'. This makes them ask, 'how is it that we hear, each in our own language in which we were born?'[11] Bewildered, they ask each other 'Whatever could this mean?' God turns untrained and rustic Galileans into fluent speakers to cover all the languages represented! And they do the job perfectly. This truly is a work of the Holy Spirit, demonstrating that He has miraculously visited His new-born church. It also underlines God's passion to extend His church, right from the start, by saving people from all over the world who will now understand the message of the cross and resurrection of the Lord Jesus Christ and trust Him as their Saviour.

Acts 2:13
Scrambled thinking: when unbelief defies logic.
Many people are compelled to accept the message that follows and publicly show, by baptism, that the Lord Jesus Christ has become their Saviour through personal faith in Him.[12] Some will need more time to get over their amazement before translating what they witnessed into personal faith. Others will realise later

that they can be forgiven and will turn to Christ. They may sincerely continue to ask, 'Whatever could this mean?' Fair enough—God expects us to think things through carefully and that can take time. Jesus Himself said, 'Seek and you will find'.[13]

But some cynics mock and suggest the preachers are drunk, claiming they have drunk too much wine. Do drunkards speak intelligently and understandably in a foreign language, especially one they have never learned? Just the reverse! A person under the influence of alcohol normally finds it hard to speak coherently in *his own* language!

What poor excuses and twisted arguments some hide behind to avoid facing their need to ask for God to forgive them for their sin. They ignore the solemn fact that life is so short. They dare not consider seriously that they are eternally lost without Christ. Although they need Jesus as their Saviour, they try to run away from Him. To cover up they treat the whole situation as a big laugh. But going to Hell is no joke. Neither was Jesus' death on the cross, when He personally suffered our deserved judgement in order to save us from sin, death and Hell.

'Fools mock at sin':[14] how very foolish to mock when forgiveness is on offer where there is serious repentance. How tragic not to repent, trust Jesus, and receive eternal life. How sad to miss the real joy, peace and blessing which the Holy Spirit brings with Him as He comes to live in our lives. Are you making excuses for not turning to Christ? I do hope not.

Questions on Chapter 3
The Day of Pentecost—Acts 2:1–13

A. What does the Holy Spirit do in this passage? Compare that with what the other verses quoted below about how the Holy Spirit works.

Acts 2:1–13, Luke 24:49, Ephesians 1:13–14, Romans 8:9–17, 1 Corinthians 12:12–13, 2 Corinthians 5:5

B. What impact would speaking perfectly in known languages, without learning them, make on (a) the foreigners in Jerusalem and (b) the Galilean Christians who witness for Christ? Do you think that what happened in Genesis 11:1–9 may be one reason why God chose this miraculous method to communicate the news about Jesus widely?
Acts 2:1–4, Mark 1:6–8, Acts 1:4–8, Acts 2:5–13, Genesis 11:1–9

C. How many reasons can you think of why people make fun of those who share the good news of Jesus Christ? Why is it foolish to do so?
Acts 2:13, Proverbs 14:9, Psalm 14:1

CHAPTER 4

What a message!

ACTS 2:14–36

¹⁴ *But Peter, standing up with the eleven, raised his voice and said to them, 'Men of Judea and all who dwell in Jerusalem, let this be known to you, and heed my words.* ¹⁵ *For these are not drunk, as you suppose, since it is only the third hour of the day.* ¹⁶ *But this is what was spoken by the prophet Joel:*

¹⁷ *"And it shall come to pass in the last days, says God,*
That I will pour out of My Spirit on all flesh;
Your sons and your daughters shall prophesy,
Your young men shall see visions,
Your old men shall dream dreams.
¹⁸ *And on My menservants and on My maidservants*
I will pour out My Spirit in those days;
And they shall prophesy.
¹⁹ *I will show wonders in heaven above*

And signs in the earth beneath:
Blood and fire and vapor of smoke.
20 *The sun shall be turned into darkness,*
And the moon into blood,
Before the coming of the great and awesome day of the Lord.
21 *And it shall come to pass*
That whoever calls on the name of the LORD
Shall be saved."

22 *'Men of Israel, hear these words: Jesus of Nazareth, a Man attested by God to you by miracles, wonders, and signs which God did through Him in your midst, as you yourselves also know—* 23 *Him, being delivered by the determined purpose and foreknowledge of God, you have taken by lawless hands, have crucified, and put to death;* 24 *whom God raised up, having loosed the pains of death, because it was not possible that He should be held by it.* 25 *For David says concerning Him:*

"I foresaw the Lord always before my face,
For He is at my right hand, that I may not be shaken.
26 *Therefore my heart rejoiced, and my tongue was glad;*
Moreover my flesh also will rest in hope.
27 *For You will not leave my soul in Hades,*
Nor will You allow Your Holy One to see corruption.
28 *You have made known to me the ways of life;*
You will make me full of joy in Your presence."

29 *'Men and brethren, let me speak freely to you of the patriarch David, that he is both dead and buried, and his tomb is with us to this day.* 30 *Therefore, being a prophet, and knowing that God had sworn with an oath to him that of the fruit of his body, according to the flesh, He would raise up the Christ to sit on his throne,* 31 *he, foreseeing this, spoke concerning the resurrection of the Christ, that His soul was not*

left in Hades, nor did His flesh see corruption. 32 This Jesus God has raised up, of which we are all witnesses. 33 Therefore being exalted to the right hand of God, and having received from the Father the promise of the Holy Spirit, He poured out this which you now see and hear.

34 'For David did not ascend into the heavens, but he says himself:

"The LORD said to my Lord,
'Sit at My right hand,
35 Till I make Your enemies Your footstool.'"'

Acts 2:14–21
This amazing event cannot be drunkenness!

Peter, with the Eleven apostles, now explains why they have spoken in other languages. But first he insists to the crowd that the speakers are not drunk. His argument is simple. *Nine in the morning* is far too early to be drunk! As someone else put it, 'People usually got drunk at night—at banquets, not at 9 a.m.; people might have a hangover in the morning, but they would hardly act drunk.'[1] Also any drunkenness at that early hour would certainly not have been on that widespread scale. And would each drunkard have achieved exactly the same remarkable result in speaking different unlearned languages fluently? To say the speakers are drunk is a 'cop-out'![2]

Peter provides the perfect explanation that God predicted would happen, through His prophet Joel.[3] The Holy Spirit would be poured out on His people. Now it is happening! Part of that prophecy says, 'whoever calls on the name of the LORD shall be saved'. The fulfilment of that, too, is on the very brink of being witnessed. The source of this gift of speaking unlearned languages fluently cannot be drunkenness: it is from the Holy Spirit.

Acts 2:22–24
These well-known facts of the gospel cannot be denied!

If Jesus Christ had lived in a giant floodlit goldfish bowl, with 24/7 detailed TV coverage, His life could scarcely have been more public than it actually was. It was recorded from four different angles in the gospels by Matthew, Mark, Luke and John. His birth, life, miracles, prayers, teaching, leadership, trials, opposition, rejection, suffering, death, resurrection, and ascension to Heaven are very well documented. It is as if these four different biographies, like four commentators covering the same football match, report the basic facts from 'each corner of the ground'. Yet they do not all mention exactly the same details surrounding those facts. Similarly the four gospels cover the same basic subject—Jesus Christ—yet without all focusing on exactly the same details. But they never contradict one another. Their accounts are therefore reliable and consistent, without being identical. How can this be? Because God the Holy Spirit is the 'master writer' who directs them, as He does all writers of the Bible.[4]

Like them, Peter also now focuses on Jesus,[5] as the One 'attested by God' for doing well-accredited 'miracles, wonders and signs'. But with the help of 'lawless hands', religious Jewish leaders manipulated the crowd to have Him 'crucified and put to death'. Peter adds that 'God raised' Him up, 'having loosed the pains of death, because it was not possible that He should be held by it'.

None of these events were done secretly in a quiet corner. It was all very public knowledge. People living at the time of Christ's cross and resurrection and near to where it all happened do not dispute the facts. It was common knowledge that Jesus died and that many people claimed to have met Him as the risen

Lord. The stubborn refusal of some to repent and believe in Jesus seems so stupid. But Jesus' disciples, like Peter, never need to argue that these events actually took place. Those there at the time knew it was true. The disciples now simply explain why. They declare that we sinners can be forgiven and *born again*[6] if we turn from our sins, believe Jesus died on the cross to take our deserved punishment, and receive Him as Lord and Saviour in our hearts. Those who do repent and receive Him are therefore converted. Their new lives demonstrate that all this really is true. These facts cannot be denied.

Acts 2:25–35
The main focus of this prophecy cannot be David!

Peter now refers his Jewish audience to Psalm 16:8–11, written by King David. Like many prophecies there is an immediate context affecting David and also a wider context to be fulfilled later. One Bible teacher said about these verses that, 'it is difficult to tell whether the crisis is past or present to the psalmist. Death may be imminent for him (v. 10).[7] David faced many crises: his life was in the balance on several occasions. But Jesus later went through a far greater crisis than any of David's: He died on the cross taking our sin and judgement.

However, His soul was never left 'in Hades'. Whereas David 'is both dead and buried and his tomb is with us to this day', he 'did not ascend into the heavens' after that. The Lord Jesus Christ has been 'raised up' and also 'exalted to the right hand of God'. He rose again never more to die.[8] He also ascended to Heaven[9] and sits on the right hand of God the Father.[10] King David knew that God had 'sworn in truth' that He would place one of his descendants on his throne as king.[11] As a Spirit-aided prophet, David knew the lasting force of this prophecy referred uniquely to Jesus, the King of kings[12] who, unlike him, would neither be held by the grave nor be subject to decay. Jesus Christ is the lasting fulfilment of these verses, as his Jewish listeners know well. The subject cannot be David, now dead and buried! Jesus is the unique, special, God-man, and the resurrected and eternal Lord and Saviour of all trusting Him personally.

Acts 2:36
The claims of Jesus Christ cannot be dismissed!

Peter's message finishes with God-given confidence and with full assurance. After all, this is God's word—not a bright idea which David somehow dreamed up. So he boldly proclaims, 'God has made this Jesus, whom you crucified, both Lord and Christ'. His hearers must now either bow their hearts, minds, wills and lives to Jesus, and plead with Him to forgive them and become their Saviour, or face eternal judgement for their sins. The same is still true for us today.[13]

That staggering offer we saw in Acts 2:21 is still open to all today: 'whoever calls on the name of the LORD shall be saved'. 'Whoever'—does that include you, do you think? Perhaps you have not yet called on the Lord Jesus Christ to forgive you and enter your life as Lord and Saviour? Or maybe you are a straying Christian who needs to call on Jesus for forgiveness, restoration and renewal?

In either case, call on Him now! Remember: the claims of the Lord Jesus Christ cannot be dismissed.

Questions on Chapter 4
What a Message!—Acts 2:14–36

A. Why are the scoffers wrong who joke that those preaching in unlearned languages are drunk. How does Peter argue

from reason and from Scripture to support his message? Who is most convincing, and why? Are there any other arguments that you would you use?
Acts 2:13, 14–20, Joel 2:28–32

B. How many separate facts about the Lord Jesus Christ can you find in Peter's message? Put down two or three words to summarise each fact you can find.
Acts 2:22–36

C. How do you link the truths in Acts 2:21 with Acts 2:36? Compare your findings with the verses below.
John 3:16, 36, 1 Peter 2:24–25, 1 Corinthians 1:18

CHAPTER 5

What a response!

ACTS 2:37–41

Now when they heard this, they were cut to the heart, and said to Peter and the rest of the apostles, 'Men and brethren, what shall we do?'

38 Then Peter said to them, 'Repent, and let every one of you be baptized in the name of Jesus Christ for the remission of sins; and you shall receive the gift of the Holy Spirit. 39 For the promise is to you and to your children, and to all who are afar off, as many as the Lord our God will call.' 40 And with many other words he testified and exhorted them, saying, 'Be saved from this perverse generation.'' 41 Then those who gladly received his word were baptized; and that day about three thousand souls were added to them.

Acts 2:37
Cut to the heart
The Holy Spirit, the *Spirit of truth*,[1] now works deeply in Peter's hearers after his message. 'Cut to the heart', they wake up to their guilt before the all-seeing God who is holy and righteous and hates sin. Sensing His coming judgement on their sins and feeling their need of forgiveness, they plead with Peter and the apostles, 'what shall we do?' Jesus had promised that the Holy Spirit would work in our lives in this way.[2]

Acts 2:38–41
Cut to the heart—and a plea to the heart
God's remedy for conscience-stricken sinners is the same today as then. Peter pleads with 'every one' of them so that they and their children can know forgiveness of their sins and so 'receive the gift of the Holy Spirit'. This good news includes '*all* who are afar off'. The Bible says, '*All* have sinned and fall short of the glory of God',[3] Christ 'died for *all*',[4] and that God 'is rich to *all* who call upon Him' for '*whoever* calls on the name of the Lord shall be saved.'.[5]

We too can know God's forgiveness and receive His 'gift of the Holy Spirit'. Our sins separate us from God[6] and make us far off from Him. But God can bring us 'near by the blood of Christ'[7] which He shed when dying for our sins. Now risen, He is 'also able to save to the uttermost those who come to God through Him, since He always lives to make intercession for them'.[8] Peter insists God will call sinners to forgiveness because 'Christ died for our sins'.[9] Is He calling you now?

Peter is very serious. He warns them 'with many other words' to be saved. This hostile world hates Christ's righteous standards, and tries to hinder anyone coming to Jesus or following Him. So

Peter's warning is, 'be saved from this perverse generation'. He tells them how: 'Repent, and let every one of you be baptized in the name of Jesus Christ for the remission of sins; and you shall receive the gift of the Holy Spirit'. God's Spirit indwells anyone trusting Christ.

Acts 2:38
Repent and be baptised

Repentance means three things: First, I admit, with shame, my sin and guilt. I confess I have offended and disobeyed or neglected God, and often have also hurt others. Second, I deliberately turn from all my sins, and ask God to forgive me. Turning from my sins will make me try to make good harm or loss I have inflicted on others, when possible.[10] Third, as forgiveness is only 'in the name of Jesus Christ', I cast myself on God's mercy by thanking Jesus for dying on the cross, where he bore my sins. As I welcome Christ into my heart as my Lord, He enters my life by the Holy Spirit to take over. The US President is more than *resident* at the White House: he is also *President*. He is the chief. Jesus enters my heart as resident and as President—or as my 'Chief'. Christ, my Saviour, died and rose again to be my *Lord*.[11] Repentance puts my life under His new management. Starting with my 'U-turn' from my sins to Christ, repentance continues daily under His guidance and direction. As I read the Bible and pray to Him I keep in daily touch with my Commander and Friend.

Baptism cannot save you. The repentant criminal dying on the cross next to Jesus[12] was never baptised, yet Jesus assured him that he would be in Paradise with Him that same day. He simply had confessed his sins sincerely and prayed to Jesus personally. The apostle Paul could not even remember whom or when he had baptised![13] He longed to see people saved by Christ.[14] He would have baptised everyone possible if baptism was essential to their being saved.

Yet baptism is commanded and important. Everyone in the Bible who trusted in Jesus after His death and resurrection is baptised. Baptism involves immersing a new Christian under water and then lifting that person out of it. It pictures outwardly what has already happened inwardly.[15] Being immersed in water demonstrates the sinner's being engulfed by sin and death. Being raised indicates God's lifting that repentant sinner to new life in Christ. It also publicly declares to the world that the baptised person now intends to live openly for Christ.[16]

Soon in Jerusalem these new Christians will be persecuted. Some will be imprisoned, others marginalised, and some killed. Their baptism announces their decision to live a new life which honours Christ,[17] whatever the cost.[18] Some orthodox Jews even held funeral services for newly converted family members. They regarded them as dead already.

So by demanding baptism Peter tests how real his hearers' repentance and personal faith in Christ is. He poses certain questions: Will you turn from your sins and give Jesus first place? Will you live a new life for Him, with His help? Will you die for Him, if necessary? Will you be known as His disciple? Are you saved? Is Christ your Lord?

'You shall receive the gift of the Holy Spirit' is God's promise made to all sinners who trust in Christ. Jesus enters our hearts through the Holy Spirit.[19] We become born-again[20] children of God.[21] The Bible says that if we have not received His Spirit, we are not His.[22] If we have, we begin to change,[23] feed spiritually, and grow. As a new-born baby has a new appetite so we now drink in the 'milk' of God's word each day.[24] The Holy Spirit desires to fill our lives continually with His presence and godly influence to produce holy and fruitful lives to glorify God.[25]

Acts 2:38–39
The Holy Spirit

The Holy Spirit is a Person, not an influence. He is also God, being One of the three Persons in the Trinity. Because He is a Person and God, we grieve him when we sin against Him. We must avoid that.[26] He is holy—the *Holy Spirit*.

He seals us. In fact He *is* the seal![27] This identifies us as Christ's and guarantees our salvation. Heaven awaits us! A seal authenticates and identifies a document. After our conversion God puts His loving hand on us as our guide, leader and friend. We are far from perfect, but we are His! As born-again Christians He has started to change us and will continue to do so until we reach eternity.

Paul told the new Philippian Christians that he was 'confident of this very thing, that He who has begun a good work in you will complete it until the day of Jesus Christ'.[28] Their faith in Christ was sealed by His obvious presence in their new lives. Jesus was their Lord and Saviour and they had received God's life-changing Holy Spirit. Have you trusted Christ? Do you know the Holy Spirit in your life? If not, will you repent from sin, and trust in Jesus? Three thousand of Peter's hearers do that now! They believe his message, yield to Christ, and are baptised. Next, we will see what they do together to help each other to go on with their new-found Saviour, and to serve Him in perilous times.

Questions on Chapter 5
What a Response!—Acts 2:37-41

    A. What is involved when a sinner who hears the good news of Jesus is 'cut to the heart' through conviction of sin? What is God's part in that? What is the sinner's part?
Acts 2:37-41, John 16:8-11

    B. Discuss the importance of the words 'every one of you' and 'all' in Acts 2:38-39 and compare that with other similar verses in the Bible.
Romans 3:23, 2 Corinthians 5:14-15, Romans 10:12-13, Joel 2:32

    C. Comparing Acts 2:38 with Acts 2:41 how do you see the link between the baptism of these new converts in Jerusalem and their repentance?
Acts 2:38, 2:41, Romans 6:1-14, Galatians 2:20

CHAPTER 6

Our first glimpse of the early church

ACTS 2:42–47

42 *And they continued steadfastly in the apostles' doctrine and fellowship, in the breaking of bread, and in prayers.* 43 *Then fear came upon every soul, and many wonders and signs were done through the apostles.* 44 *Now all who believed were together, and had all things in common,* 45 *and sold their possessions and goods, and divided them among all, as anyone had need.*

46 *So continuing daily with one accord in the temple, and breaking bread from house to house, they ate their food with gladness and simplicity of heart,* 47 *praising God and having favor with all the people. And the Lord added to the church daily those who were being saved.*

Acts 2:42
Meet the very first church

Some people think the 'church' is a boring religious club, or an old building, or just an organisation. Seen as being out of touch, out of date, and irrelevant, they think the sooner it closes down, the better. These early Christians might agree! Happily, although some churches are like that, it is not true of others. These early Christians were certainly different! The changed lives of those who put their trust in Jesus Christ amazed everyone, including themselves.

This first church in history, run by responsible Christian leaders,[1] is a pattern for all churches today. The church is people: converted and changed people; people enthusiastic about their new relationship with God. Jesus Christ is their foundation and cornerstone.[2] They want get to know Him better, to live to please Him, and to help others. These men and women have turned from wrongdoing and asked Jesus Christ to save them. He has done that. He died on the cross to take their judgement for that wrongdoing. He lives today and, through the Holy Spirit, gives them a new inner joy and enthusiasm for living. That will continue when they soon face cruel opposition, merciless persecution, imprisonment and death. Have they committed horrible crimes? No! They simply have taken the Lord Jesus Christ as their Lord, Saviour, Master, Friend and King. They now live to please and serve Him!

How to get God's help to carry on as a Christian

Without Christ in their lives, they could not live like that, nor even want to! So God has given four helps for them to make progress, while enjoying their new peace and satisfaction found in knowing Jesus. What are those four helps?

God's first help: God's word, or the Bible, or the apostles' doctrine

Christians are newly born-again 'babes' needing the milk of God's word.[3] The whole Bible, namely the Old and New Testaments, is God's inspired, faultless and complete word, called here 'the apostles' doctrine'.[4] The Bible is a Holy Spirit inspired library of sixty-six books, all accurate and trustworthy. Anyone seeking truth should read it each day.[5] The Old Testament's thirty-nine books begin with creation. They trace God's dealings with people, and their responses, until Jesus Christ was born in Bethlehem about two thousand years ago. The New Testament's twenty-seven books cover the birth, life, miracles, teaching, suffering, death, resurrection and ascension to Heaven of Jesus. They describe the events before Jesus returns in glory to end this world and bring in a perfect New Heaven and Earth.[6] They focus on how sinners can be forgiven and receive eternal life. Read the Bible carefully and ask God to help you and bless you through it. Mark's gospel is one good starting point.[7]

God's second help: sharing, or fellowship with other believers

The second help is fellowship. This word literally means 'sharing'. The new believers share together their time, blessings, problems, prayers, and efforts to help others to come to know their Saviour. Their new unity, often with people unknown or hardly known before, makes them into a family. They are open, honest, caring and generous. They love to meet together. Because regular Christian fellowship still helps many today we are warned not to forsake it.[8] In becoming children of God by receiving Christ[9] we discover 'new' brothers and sisters in Christ, with God as our Father.[10] The Bible rightly says 'you are all one in Christ'.[11]

God's third help: Holy Communion, the Lord's Supper, the Lord's Table or the breaking of bread

The third activity, 'the breaking of bread', takes on real meaning to anyone coming to know Christ. Also known as 'Holy Communion', 'The Lord's Table' or 'The Lord's Supper' it is a simple remembrance, recorded in the Bible, that in dying on the cross, Jesus' body was broken for us and His blood was shed[12] for our sins. This simple remembrance shows that the Jewish Passover was fulfilled in the death on the cross of Jesus Christ, our 'Passover lamb'.[13] Every Lord's Day (Sunday) believers across the world remember this and share fellowship with others. This act of remembrance is to be kept until Christ comes again in glory and power. It looks forward to that great climactic event as well as looking back to the cross where the Saviour died in our place.[14]

God's fourth help: Prayer

Prayer always helps Christians. It is never out of date and crosses all boundaries. These new converts discover the reality of personal prayer and meet to pray and share together and with God. Paul urged the Philippians, 'Be anxious for nothing, but in everything by prayer and supplication, with thanksgiving, let your requests be made known to God; and the peace of God, which surpasses all understanding, will guard your hearts and minds through Christ Jesus'.[15] Prayer is talking to God and letting your requests be made known to Him. Supplication is humbly asking specific things from God, for others and for yourself with a sense of unworthiness and to honour Him. Thanksgiving pleases God as He listens to His thankful children. Praying with fellow-believers in Christ is a wonderful discovery to make!

Acts 2:44–47
Awesome! Then see what happened next!

'Then fear came upon every soul'[16] Meanwhile God continues to give 'many wonders and signs' through His apostles. Everyone can see that these men act with His authority and power as His chosen channels.[17] The Holy Spirit will complete the New Testament and therefore His written word, the Bible, through these apostles.[18] As well as the awe and the apostles' wonders and miraculous signs, God is at work in each new Christian. He is changing them deeply as individuals, and together they form a unique group of people. Such is the positive impact of their new lives, and their shared message of eternal life through personal faith in Christ, that 'the Lord added to the church *daily* [my emphasis] those who were being saved'.

Although persecution will come, those who are near to them now see what is happening and are convinced. So what do onlookers see in these people who have recently received Christ? First, an unplanned and joyful togetherness leads to selfless sharing of what they have with each other.[19] Next, they sacrificially sell their own 'possessions and goods' to give to people in 'need'.[20] They are continually motivated for this by their daily Christian meetings 'in the temple'. Hospitality with 'gladness and simplicity of heart' provides food and fellowship to all in their homes.[21] Their ongoing 'praising God' for how His wonderful gospel has changed them is probably the springboard for everything else they do. Is it any wonder that such a magnetic and gracious change in them causes them to enjoy 'having favour with all the people'?[22]

Questions on Chapter 6
Our First Glimpse of the Early Church—Acts 2:42–47

A. Why is it important that Christians read, study and hear God's word (the *apostles' teaching*)? Why is the Bible such a help to Christians?
Acts 2:42, 2 Timothy 2:15, 2 Timothy 3:16, Psalm 119:105

B. Discuss the other three ways in which God helps the believers in the early church, and why these three helps are so important to Christians and to churches today.
Hebrews 10:25, 1 Corinthians 11:27–28, Philippians 4:6–7

C. 'Then fear [awe] came upon every soul' says Acts 2:43. How is this awesome experience expressed in the way the new Christians live as seen in Acts 2:44–47? Even though we live in different times today, how can the principles on which they lived be followed by Christians in today's world?

CHAPTER 7

A brand new walk

ACTS 3:1–10

¹ *Now Peter and John went up together to the temple at the hour of prayer, the ninth* hour. ² *And a certain man lame from his mother's womb was carried, whom they laid daily at the gate of the temple which is called Beautiful, to ask alms from those who entered the temple;* ³ *who, seeing Peter and John about to go into the temple, asked for alms.* ⁴ *And fixing his eyes on him, with John, Peter said, 'Look at us.'* ⁵ *So he gave them his attention, expecting to receive something from them.* ⁶ *Then Peter said, 'Silver and gold I do not have, but what I do have I give you: In the name of Jesus Christ of Nazareth, rise up and walk.'* ⁷ *And he took him by the right hand and lifted him up, and immediately his feet and ankle bones received strength.* ⁸ *So he, leaping up, stood and walked and entered the temple with them—walking, leaping, and praising God.* ⁹ *And all the people saw him walking and praising God.* ¹⁰ *Then they knew that it was he*

who sat begging alms at the Beautiful Gate of the temple; and they were filled with wonder and amazement at what had happened to him.

Acts 3:1–5
A lame beggar asks for 'alms'—and gets legs!
Peter and John now use the power the Holy Spirit gives to the apostles to heal.[1] This emphasises the authority God gives them to preach the good news about Jesus Christ. It is 3 o'clock in the afternoon.[2] As they approach the Temple to pray they pass by the 'Beautiful Gate' of the Temple.

For an unnamed beggar, lame from birth, today is just another normal sad day. Others placed him there again to beg. He hopes for money or food from kind passers-by.[3] Perhaps this beggar feels that God-fearing Jews going to pray in the Temple are an 'easy touch' for him. He is more likely to receive sympathy—and cash—from believers in God like them than from others.

As he asks the two apostles to give him something, they gaze at him. Peter says 'Look at us'. Any rising hopes he has of charity are immediately dashed, however, by Peter's next sentence! 'Silver and gold I do not have'. But before disappointment can settle in the poor beggar's sad mind, the apostle suggests something much better!

Acts 3:6
An unexpected offer
Peter starts by making it clear that it is only 'in the name of Jesus Christ' that he can make his offer which is more valuable than silver and gold The lame beggar has, no doubt, often heard passers-by discussing Jesus Christ. His matchless teaching, staggering miracles, and His claims to be God in the flesh have been on everyone's lips. But His death on Calvary's cross, and

the claims of many folk that they have met Jesus since then, now risen from the dead, is still a main topic of conversation. So is all this talk about Galileans speaking foreign languages perfectly and without a trace of an accent. As a 'Temple beggar' he probably heard that the thick veil, separating the Temple's holy place from the most holy place, was recently torn in two from top to bottom as Jesus died.[4] If so, has he worked out that the way to God is now open to all sinners because Jesus died and bore our sins in His own body on the cross?[5]

But what does Peter now offer him in the name of Jesus? 'In the name of Jesus Christ—walk!' What did he say? *Walk*? After all this time—*walk*? Yes! *Walk*! 'In the name of Jesus Christ—walk!'

Acts 3:7–8
A miraculous result

Peter knows very well that only Jesus can work this miracle to make the lame man walk. But he wants to encourage him to respond by putting his faith in Christ as his Lord and Saviour. Peter grabs his right hand and helps him up.

Who is most excited by the immediate and miraculous result? Is it the beggar or the two apostles? With newly strengthened feet and ankles the 'lame' beggar now leaps, stands, and walks. He then enters the Temple with them. Can anyone witnessing this amazing act of God doubt Jesus Christ's power, or the truth of the gospel preached by His apostles? It's as if this miracle insists to all, 'You must believe in the risen Jesus: you must trust the message of forgiveness through His death on the cross that these men bring to you.'

But the miracle also illustrates how God works to change us. Our sins have disabled us morally: we cannot walk in His righteous ways. We are morally and spiritually lame and powerless.

We cannot cure ourselves or save ourselves. Nor can any religion put us right, even if it is called 'Christian'. Only trusting the Lord Jesus Christ personally can make the difference!

The name, *Jesus* means *God saves*. To believe in His name, means we believe He can save us from our sins.[6] He alone can forgive our sins, enter our lives through the Holy Spirit, and enable us to walk a new walk with Him. Jesus walked to the cross to bear our sins and punishment. He walked in His resurrection power with the two sad travellers to Emmaus[7] and changed them completely. Jesus enables those who receive Him into their hearts by faith also to walk with Him by faith.[8] Just as the ex-beggar leaps for joy, stands straight, and goes to a place of worship along with Jesus' disciples to praise God there, so we too can know His 'joy inexpressible and full of glory',[9] stand straight morally, and worshipfully praise the Lord who has saved us and blessed us! It is a miracle of God's grace.

Acts 3:9–10
An immediate impact

I wonder what the average Temple-goer thinks in that Temple court as he looks on. May we use our imaginations?

> What is all that commotion? I wanted some peace and quiet here in the Temple! But who is that guy jumping all over the place and shouting 'Praise the Lord!'? Didn't those two guys with him speak in those other languages at Pentecost? Didn't one of them tell us to repent and trust Jesus Christ? My mates said they were drunk, but they seemed sober to me.
>
> Hang on! He's that lame Temple beggar from the Beautiful Gate! He's often asked me for money! But how can it be? A few minutes ago I saw him begging at that gate again. I'm off to ask

those two what it's all about. Perhaps I can also get some sense out of that lame—well 'unlame' now—beggar. But he seems too happy to talk sense right now!

The crowd is absolutely staggered, very impressed, but completely bewildered by the change in the once-lame beggar. So today, when the watching world sees a surprising change in a man or woman, which is different but just as striking as for that beggar, it is speechless. When selfish, dishonest, and immoral people suddenly change direction and start talking enthusiastically about Jesus, it is hard to understand, unless you have experienced the same blessing.

Charlie was a young violent inmate in a London prison. In his violent mood he said, 'I would do anything'. During his long sentence he attended a weekly Bible study. After a few weeks he trusted Christ as his Saviour. He was transferred to another prison. An experienced staff member there could not understand his violent criminal record, such is the amazing change in him in a few months. Charlie explains: 'I trusted Jesus as my Saviour. I felt dead inside before. Now I am alive!' Fellow prisoners try to work out how he 'ticks'. Unless Jesus changes them too, they may never know.

I felt like that when my sister's life changed after she received Christ. I told her defiantly, 'It will never happen to me'. The rest is history! Jesus saved me and is changing me still. Do you know anyone whose life has been turned upside down—or, rather, the right way up—by personal faith in Christ? Jesus described this change as being *born again*.[10]

The Bible says, 'if anyone is in Christ, he is a new creation; old things have passed away; behold, all things have become new'.[11] Going through religious observances or doing our best can never save us from our sins.[12] Becoming 'a new creation' in Christ does. This radical personal change within comes when you own up to your sin, turn from it, and surrender your heart to Christ. With your past forgiven, your life changed, and Heaven to come, you know you have been 'born again'. Are *you* born again? You can be if you believe in Jesus Christ to save you.[13]

Questions on Chapter 7
A Brand New Walk—Acts 3:1–10

A. Consider the lame beggar. How does his miraculous healing help to further the work of the gospel? How does it also illustrate what a new walk with God through Christ means?
Acts 3:9–10, 3:12, Colossians 2:6–7, Ephesians 5:8, 1 John 1:6–7

B. What part did (a) Peter and John and (b) the beggar himself play in the miraculous healing. What did God do that they could never do? What parallels can you find between this healing and a sinner coming to faith in Christ?
Acts 3:1–7, Acts 16:28–33

C. Imagine you are looking on as the healed beggar leaps past you in the Temple area. What three things do you think would impress you most, and why? What can a Christian today do to influence others for the good news of Jesus Christ? How can that happen?
Acts 3:6–10, Matthew 5:16, 2 Corinthians 4:1–6

CHAPTER 8

Peter preaches again

ACTS 3:11–26

¹¹ *Now as the lame man who was healed held on to Peter and John, all the people ran together to them in the porch which is called Solomon's, greatly amazed.* ¹² *So when Peter saw it, he responded to the people: 'Men of Israel, why do you marvel at this? Or why look so intently at us, as though by our own power or godliness we had made this man walk?* ¹³ *The God of Abraham, Isaac, and Jacob, the God of our fathers, glorified His Servant Jesus, whom you delivered up and denied in the presence of Pilate, when he was determined to let Him go.* ¹⁴ *But you denied the Holy One and the Just, and asked for a murderer to be granted to you,* ¹⁵ *and killed the Prince of life, whom God raised from the dead, of which we are witnesses.* ¹⁶ *And His name, through faith in His name, has made this man strong, whom you see and know. Yes, the faith which comes through Him has given him this perfect soundness in the presence of you all.*

[17] 'Yet now, brethren, I know that you did it in ignorance, as did also your rulers. [18] But those things which God foretold by the mouth of all His prophets, that the Christ would suffer, He has thus fulfilled. [19] Repent therefore and be converted, that your sins may be blotted out, so that times of refreshing may come from the presence of the Lord, [20] and that He may send Jesus Christ, who was preached to you before, [21] whom heaven must receive until the times of restoration of all things, which God has spoken by the mouth of all His holy prophets since the world began. [22] For Moses truly said to the fathers, "The LORD your God will raise up for you a Prophet like me from your brethren. Him you shall hear in all things, whatever He says to you. [23] And it shall be that every soul who will not hear that Prophet shall be utterly destroyed from among the people."[24] Yes, and all the prophets, from Samuel and those who follow, as many as have spoken, have also foretold these days. [25] You are sons of the prophets, and of the covenant which God made with our fathers, saying to Abraham, "And in your seed all the families of the earth shall be blessed." [26] To you first, God, having raised up His Servant Jesus, sent Him to bless you, in turning away every one of you from your iniquities.'

Acts 3:11–12
A ready-made audience

Curious and excited, the people swarm to the Temple porch. Peter takes the opportunity to speak about the healed man. Still more important, he explains about the Lord Jesus Christ. He draws no attention to himself, the channel of God's blessing, but to his Saviour who is the source of it. He stresses that neither John nor he possesses their own 'power or godliness' to heal the lame beggar. God alone can bless!

His second spontaneous sermon now covers basically the same ground as his first. The gospel is unchangeable! It should include the main points which Peter focuses on now. Verses 13 to 26, give a summary of his sermon, not the details of it.

Acts 3:13–26
Peter's sermon in a nutshell
We will now look at the main points covered by Peter's sermon.
- God whom we talk about is the same God trusted by Israel's fathers, Abraham, Isaac and Jacob. (Acts 3:13)
- Jesus, God's Son, is also His Servant. He is now glorified after His resurrection and ascension. (Acts 3:13–15)
- You, the listening crowd, are responsible for Christ's death, through cowardly Pilate. You preferred a convicted murderer to Jesus, the 'Prince of life'. (Acts 3:13–15)
- We witnessed personally that Jesus, the One you caused to die, really did rise from the dead. (Acts 3:15)
- Through the lame man's faith in Jesus' name he is healed. You all are witnessing that right now. (Acts 3:16)
- Just like your rulers, your sin caused you to act ignorantly. (Acts 3:17)
- The Old Testament foretold why Jesus must suffer, die, and rise again. (Acts 3:18 & 3:21–26)
- God did this for you: you must repent and be turned from your sins to the risen Christ in order to know God's blessings now and eternally. (Acts 3:19–20 & 3:26)

Consider those last two points in more detail.

Acts 3:18 & 3:21–26
Isaiah and David, moved by the Holy Spirit, speak about Jesus as the suffering Servant
Isaiah 52:13–53:12 is a 'must read' Old Testament passage of God's word. Peter quotes from it in 1 Peter 2:24–25 when he says that

Jesus Christ 'Himself bore our sins in His own body on the tree, that we, having died to sins, might live for righteousness—by whose stripes you were healed. For you were like sheep going astray, but have now returned to the Shepherd and Overseer of your souls'. In Acts 8:26 an Ethiopian treasurer, a convert to Judaism, returns home from worshipping in Jerusalem. In his chariot he reads from Isaiah chapter 53. Philip, sent by God to speak to the Ethiopian, tells him about Jesus from that chapter.[1] The New Testament shows that this passage deals with Jesus and his death and resurrection.[2] In Psalm 22, another 'must read' Old Testament chapter, David describes Christ's crucifixion in detail many years before death by crucifixion was even practised![3]

As Peter now speaks he has these passages in mind. They are 'those things which God foretold by the mouth of all His prophets, that the Christ would suffer'. These are things 'He has thus fulfilled'. Verses 15 and 26 clearly show that Peter has Jesus's resurrection and ascension in mind. Peter knows that Isaiah prophesied that Jesus 'shall be exalted and extolled and be very high'.[4] These and other Bible passages teach that Jesus has borne our sins and been punished there in our place for them. Isaiah 53:3–6 says:

> *He is despised and rejected by men,*
> *A Man of sorrows and acquainted with grief.*
> *And we hid, as it were, our faces from Him;*
> *He was despised, and we did not esteem Him.*
> *4 Surely He has borne our griefs*
> *And carried our sorrows;*
> *Yet we esteemed Him stricken,*
> *Smitten by God, and afflicted.*
> *5 But He was wounded for our transgressions,*
> *He was bruised for our iniquities;*

Peter preaches again—Acts 3:11–26

> *The chastisement for our peace was upon Him,*
> *And by His stripes we are healed.*
> *⁶ All we like sheep have gone astray;*
> *We have turned, every one, to his own way;*
> *And the Lord has laid on Him the iniquity of us all.*

The crowd had probably never considered that the Lord Jesus Christ had carried their sins and their deserved punishment for them. Have *you* ever realised that Christ's death was for *you*?

Acts 3:19–20 & 3:26
The challenge which brings double blessing!

Verses 20 and 21 deal with the glorious second coming of the Lord Jesus Christ, and why we must listen to Him as God's supreme and final 'Prophet'.[5] Jesus also fulfils other amazing roles![6] We face judgement if we neglect or reject what He says. But the verses also teach how we can be part of God's forgiven worldwide family by faith. Put verses 19–20 and 26 together to apply Peter's challenging message, and claim the promise of *double* blessing!

> ¹⁹ *Repent therefore and be converted, that your sins may be blotted out, so that times of refreshing may come from the presence of the Lord,* ²⁰ *and that He may send Jesus Christ, who was preached to you before.*

> ²⁶ *To you first, God, having raised up His Servant Jesus, sent Him to bless you, in turning away every one of you from your iniquities.*

Originally, English education was based on reading, writing and arithmetic. That combination was humorously called 'the three "R"s', namely reading, 'riting and 'rithmetic! God has 'three Rs' of blessing for you through Christ: *Repent* from sin, *Return* to God through faith in the crucified and risen Christ, and receive God's *Refreshing* double blessing of forgiveness in your life. Why is this a double blessing for all who repent and trust Jesus? First, it turns you from your sins which otherwise will spoil your life and others' lives. Second, by turning you to Christ, you receive forgiveness and eternal life now. They continue, after death, forever in Heaven!

We all need Christ and His double blessing. There are no exceptions.[7] We all have sinned. We must all face judgement unless we trust Christ. Christ died to pay a 'ransom for all'.[8] He offers to save all who come to Him.[9] That is why verse 26 says God wants to turn 'every one of you from your iniquities'.

Have *you* repented and come to Him? Has He turned *you* from your wicked ways? Has He ransomed *you*? Are *you* restored to God through faith in Christ? Are *you* being refreshed by the amazing blessing of knowing Jesus as your Lord and Saviour?

Questions on Chapter 8
Peter Preaches Again—Acts 3:11–26

A. What can you learn from Peter about how wisely to take an opportunity to speak for Christ?
   Acts 3:11–12, Acts 4:2, 2 Timothy 4:2

B. What place has the Old Testament here in the thinking of the apostles about the death, resurrection and ascension of the Lord Jesus Christ?
   Acts 3:13–26, Isaiah 52:13–53:12, Psalm 22

C. Consider the word 'refreshing'. Who and what bring refreshing to sinners and how?
   Acts 3:19, 26, Matthew 11:28–30, Isaiah 40:31

CHAPTER 9

In custody and in court

ACTS 4:1–12

¹ *Now as they spoke to the people, the priests, the captain of the temple, and the Sadducees came upon them,* ² *being greatly disturbed that they taught the people and preached in Jesus the resurrection from the dead.* ³ *And they laid hands on them, and put them in custody until the next day, for it was already evening.* ⁴ *However, many of those who heard the word believed; and the number of the men came to be about five thousand.* ⁵ *And it came to pass, on the next day, that their rulers, elders, and scribes,* ⁶ *as well as Annas the high priest, Caiaphas, John, and Alexander, and as many as were of the family of the high priest, were gathered together at Jerusalem.* ⁷ *And when they had set them in the midst, they asked, 'By what power or by what name have you done this?'*

⁸ *Then Peter, filled with the Holy Spirit, said to them, 'Rulers of the people and elders of Israel:* ⁹ *If we this day are judged for a good*

deed done to a helpless man, by what means he has been made well, ¹⁰ *let it be known to you all, and to all the people of Israel, that by the name of Jesus Christ of Nazareth, whom you crucified, whom God raised from the dead, by Him this man stands here before you whole.* ¹¹ *This is the "stone which was rejected by you builders, which has become the chief cornerstone."* ¹² *Nor is there salvation in any other, for there is no other name under heaven given among men by which we must be saved.'*

Acts 4:1–3
Locked up!

The priests, scribes and religious leaders had opposed Jesus and shouted for His blood.[1] Now they approach the apostles with the captain of the temple guard. He is probably hoping for a quiet life on temple duty. He does not want to have his peace shattered. The Sadducees—the anti-resurrection party[2]—serve with the Pharisees in the Council of Jewish religious leaders. Although believing in resurrection, they detest the thought of strong and well-attested evidence that *Jesus* has risen from the dead. They are worried to hear it being preached with authority and conviction as a key part of God's message of forgiveness through Christ alone.

The priests, temple guard and Sadducees are greatly disturbed this evening to see in their own temple so many listening attentively to the message of forgiveness and new life in the *risen* Saviour, whom they caused to be crucified. They seize Peter and John and put them in jail for at least an overnight stay. What a day this has been for the apostles!

Acts 4:4
Five thousand believers
That is a bit like locking the stable door after the horse has bolted! Imprisoning the preachers cannot bind the message they have proclaimed. Many have already heard it. Five thousand men believe in Christ in that Jewish temple. However strong the opposition, people turn to Jesus as Saviour when the good news of His death and resurrection is shared.

Acts 4:5–8
Peter proves you can trust Christ's promise
Speaking of the end times, but relevant to all times, Jesus had warned His disciples 'But watch out for yourselves, for they will deliver you up to councils, and you will be beaten in the synagogues. You will be brought before rulers and kings for My sake, for a testimony to them. And the gospel must first be preached to all the nations. But when they arrest you and deliver you up, do not worry beforehand, or premeditate what you will speak. But whatever is given you in that hour, speak that; for it is not you who speak, but the Holy Spirit'.[3]

Now two uneducated apostles face the might of the Jerusalem Council, without any legal representation or preparation. The experienced dignitaries gathered there include the high priest, Caiaphas, and his predecessor Annas. John and Alexander, also of high-priestly descent, are also present. This is the Council's 'A team' of biased and hostile interrogators who surround the two Christian men. Their grilling begins with: 'By what power or by what name have you done this?' This is the very hour when the apostles need to know that 'it is not you who speak, but the Holy Spirit'.[4] The promise of Jesus kicks in for them just when they need Him. 'Then Peter, *filled with the Holy Spirit*, said to them, 'Rulers of the people and elders of Israel …'

Still the same clear message

Peter had been ashamed, fearful and cowardly in his earlier denials of Jesus. Now his Spirit-given boldness and clarity mean he is by no means overawed. He knows who his hearers are and is aware of the possible fatal consequences for him and for John.

He cleverly points out that the healed man has received a real benefit and has been made well. What crime could that possibly constitute? He then answers directly the question asked. Perhaps, during their night in custody, John and he prayed for such an opportunity to proclaim their Saviour to such needy yet influential people! He says, 'let it be known to you all, and to all the people of Israel'. This is no longer the language of an ashamed coward.

Without apology he declares that the man has been healed through the name and power of 'Jesus Christ of Nazareth'. But he says more! The two truths they hate to hear are 'you crucified' Jesus but 'God raised [Him] from the dead'. Can you wonder why later their fellow apostle, Paul, tells the Christians at Corinth that the most important twin truths of the gospel are 'Christ died for our sins according to the Scriptures, and that He was buried, and that He rose again the third day according to the Scriptures'?[5]

This is probably only a short summary of how Peter responds. Doubtless he follows the apostles' practice of pointing out that Jesus died a sacrificial death as the Lamb of God and bore our sins and judgement in His body in our place on that cross. How can he fail to proclaim that God the Father accepted the finished sacrifice of Christ for guilty sinners and showed that was so by raising Him from the dead?

He goes on to present Jesus as the 'chief corner stone' in God's 'building' of salvation and forgiveness. Without the crucified and risen Jesus, God's eternal forgiveness could not be on offer. With Him as our Saviour our certainty of forgiveness is rock solid forever.

If those truths offend the pride and convict the lost religious hearts of those opposing the gospel, there is something else to come! Peter insists that there is no salvation 'in any other, for there is no other name under heaven given among men by which we must be saved.' Peter no doubt remembers how Jesus answered Thomas' question, 'How can we know the way?' with His classic and wonderfully dogmatic statement, 'I am the way, the truth, and the life. No one comes to the Father except through Me'.[6] Today, we still need to hear that clearly.

So, helped by God, Peter replies honestly and clearly from the heart, from the shoulder, and from the teaching of the Lord Jesus Christ Himself. That is how to present the Christian message.

Has 'the penny dropped' yet for you, that you *must* trust Jesus as your Saviour to avoid being lost eternally? You cannot be 'saved' otherwise. Do you realise that just as you are included in the *whoever* in the verse which says 'Whoever calls on the name of the LORD shall be saved', so you are also included in the *no one* in the verse clarifying that 'no one comes to the Father except through Me?'[7]

Questions on Chapter 9
In Custody and in Court—Acts 4:1–12

A. What potential problems do Peter and John face in Acts 4:1–7 and how are they helped to deal with them? How can we be helped in difficult situations of this nature?
Acts 4:1–7, Mark 13:9–11, Philippians 4:13, Hebrews 13:5–6, James 1:5

B. Compare Peter's message here with his other messages so far in Acts. What should be the main focus of our gospel message?
Acts 4:10–12, Acts 2:14–38, Acts 3:12–26, 1 Corinthians 15:3–4, 1 Corinthians 2:2

C. Why is it so logical, reasonable and scriptural that a sinner can only be saved by faith in the Lord Jesus Christ?
Acts 4:12, John 14:6, 1 Timothy 1:15, Hebrews 7:25, 1 Corinthians 1:21

Chapter 10

Prejudice, priority, prayer and practice

Acts 4:13–37

¹³ *Now when they saw the boldness of Peter and John, and perceived that they were uneducated and untrained men, they marveled. And they realized that they had been with Jesus.* ¹⁴ *And seeing the man who had been healed standing with them, they could say nothing against it.* ¹⁵ *But when they had commanded them to go aside out of the council, they conferred among themselves,* ¹⁶ *saying, 'What shall we do to these men? For, indeed, that a notable miracle has been done through them is evident to all who dwell in Jerusalem, and we cannot deny it.* ¹⁷ *But so that it spreads no further among the people, let us severely threaten them, that from now on they speak to no man in this name.'*

¹⁸ *So they called them and commanded them not to speak at all nor teach in the name of Jesus.* ¹⁹ *But Peter and John answered and said to them, 'Whether it is right in the sight of God to listen to you more*

than to God, you judge.' 20 For we cannot but speak the things which we have seen and heard.' 21 So when they had further threatened them, they let them go, finding no way of punishing them, because of the people, since they all glorified God for what had been done. 22 For the man was over forty years old on whom this miracle of healing had been performed. 23 And being let go, they went to their own companions and reported all that the chief priests and elders had said to them. 24 So when they heard that, they raised their voice to God with one accord and said: 'Lord, You are God, who made heaven and earth and the sea, and all that is in them, 25 who by the mouth of Your servant David have said:

"Why did the nations rage,
And the people plot vain things?
26 The kings of the earth took their stand,
And the rulers were gathered together
Against the LORD and against His Christ."

27 'For truly against Your holy Servant Jesus, whom You anointed, both Herod and Pontius Pilate, with the Gentiles and the people of Israel, were gathered together 28 to do whatever Your hand and Your purpose determined before to be done. 29 Now, Lord, look on their threats, and grant to Your servants that with all boldness they may speak Your word, 30 by stretching out Your hand to heal, and that signs and wonders may be done through the name of Your holy Servant Jesus.'

31 And when they had prayed, the place where they were assembled together was shaken; and they were all filled with the Holy Spirit, and they spoke the word of God with boldness.

32 Now the multitude of those who believed were of one heart and one soul; neither did anyone say that any of the things he possessed was his

own, but they had all things in common. 33 And with great power the apostles gave witness to the resurrection of the Lord Jesus. And great grace was upon them all. 34 Nor was there anyone among them who lacked; for all who were possessors of lands or houses sold them, and brought the proceeds of the things that were sold, 35 and laid them at the apostles' feet; and they distributed to each as anyone had need.

36 And Joses, who was also named Barnabas by the apostles (which is translated Son of Encouragement), a Levite of the country of Cyprus, 37 having land, sold it, and brought the money and laid it at the apostles' feet.

Acts 4:13–18
Prejudiced? Convinced? Changed?

The prejudiced Council leaders are given the opportunity to rethink their position, to reset their moral compass, and even to enter into the blessing of accepting the apostles' message and turning to Christ for forgiveness. Will they be convinced and change their position? Or are their minds like concrete: all mixed up and permanently set? One rhyme says, 'A man convinced against his will is of the same opinion still.'

Why should they change their minds? There are four main reasons.

First, they know that the temple veil between the holy place and the most holy place was torn from top to bottom, as Jesus died on the cross. This signalled that through Christ crucified the way was now open to know God. It was one of several miracles which accompanied Calvary.[1] God ensured that no one should forget the day that His Son died.

Second, they are well aware that the evidence for the resurrection of Jesus is watertight. Many and varied first hand, credible, corroborated witnesses—friends and foes of Christianity—confirm it is so.[2]

Third, they cannot explain how the two 'uneducated and untrained men', Peter and John, can speak with such composure, confidence, clarity and authority under such personal pressure. They recognise that they 'had been with Jesus'. They can see what a huge difference that has made to the apostles.

Fourth, they have to admit to each other that in the healing of the lame beggar 'a notable miracle has been done' and cannot be denied. The only evidence, plentiful as it is, and the only explanation given are that this healing came only by faith in the name of Jesus.

Should they not therefore, turn to Jesus themselves and urge others to do so? Why do they not turn from their own sins, thank Jesus for dying for them on the cross, and put their faith in that amazing Person and in His name? Is that what they do?

No! It is not! They do not revere and trust in the name of Jesus. Instead, they oppose it. They are determined to stop it spreading any further, in spite of all the blessing which has come through that name. Such is their guilt and spiritual blindness that they agree together to warn Peter and John not to 'speak at all nor teach in the name of Jesus'. Today, Christians face similar opposition worldwide. It can come from individuals, other religions, atheists, evolutionists, those with a different moral agenda, and ungodly authorities. Even in some countries which owe much to the hugely beneficial effect of Jesus Christ on their society, the anti-Christian cry is heard. Some hypocritically oppose free speech by Christians on some matters but uphold it for anyone else! How like the Jerusalem Council.

Do you oppose Jesus? Or do you just try to ignore Him, or delay responding to Him in repentance and personal faith? He is not your enemy! Recognise Him as the potential 'Friend who sticks closer than a brother.'[3] for all who turn from their sins and trust in Him. He wants to bless you, not harm you. Put your fears behind you and pray to Him.

Acts 4:19–22
Priority Preaching
Peter's and John's priority now is to offer God's forgiveness of sins and eternal life to all who will do a 'U turn' from sin and come to Christ as Saviour. Eventually this priority, and their faithful preaching, will cost Peter his life and John his freedom.[4] Now they ask the Council of supposedly moral religious men to judge whether the two of them should obey the Council or God. In today's popular phrase, that is a 'no brainer' to them! They must obey God and stay faithful to His word: they have made their choice.

The cowardly Council dare not punish them. Why? First, the two men have done no wrong (which is a gross understatement); and second, the religious leaders are scared of violent public reaction if they punish Peter and John. The people know what has happened to this lame beggar in his forties and glorify God for it.

Never think that being religious, even being a religious leader, means a person is forgiven or knows God. A Christian is a guilty sinner, forgiven and changed solely by trusting Jesus. He is 'the way, the truth, and the life',[5] and the only Saviour.

Acts 4:23–31
Praying people
Peter and John leave the Council's corrupt court and join their Christian friends at a prayer meeting! They report back there.

They are encouraged by reading from a Psalm about God's power as Creator and about the coming of Christ, despite powerful opposition.[6] They pray for God's will to be done, that He will note the threats against them, and enable them nevertheless to speak the Lord's word 'with all boldness'. Boldness characterises the New Testament Spirit-filled church. Christians need Holy Spirit boldness today! In these early days of the church, they pray that God will convince those hearing the gospel message, by granting healings, signs and wonders through the despised name of 'Your holy Servant Jesus'. God answers their prayers, not now with tongues like fire or with speaking foreign languages. God shakes the place where they gather, fills them with His Holy Spirit, and again they 'spoke the word of God with *boldness*'. Obviously we need to be sensible, sensitive and wise, but we do need His boldness to witness too!

Acts 4:32–37
Generous people

The new believers not only share God's message with others. They also share themselves and what they have with each other and with needy people. Some voluntarily sell their property and use the twelve apostles to distribute it wisely to support the needy. A Levite[7] from Cyprus, called Joses and later called Barnabas, does this. Barnabas means *son of encouragement*. We will see later that he lives up to his name.

Community living is not a requirement for all Christians or for all time. Circumstances and cultures change. Perhaps some of those who now benefit from community living are refugees and include widows. But generosity towards and care for others still apply, and mark out a person whose heart has been changed by Christ. Jesus can make a mean man generous and a selfish woman care for others.

If Christ is Lord of our hearts, His lordship will extend to our wallets, cheque books, credit cards, and hospitality. Because we have received so much from Jesus we should be generous too. Jesus said, 'It is more blessed to give than to receive' and 'Freely you have received, freely give'.[8] Again much wisdom and common sense must be applied in following this through, but the expectation to be generous is laid upon those who have already received the free but invaluable gift of eternal life![9]

Questions on Chapter 10
Prejudice, Priority, Prayer and Practice—Acts 4:13–37

A. How reasonable is the opposition of the Council to the apostles and their message? How do Peter and John deal with their hostility?
Acts 4:13–22, Isaiah 53:3, John 15:18, 2 Timothy 3:12, 1 Peter 3:15–17

B. What are the main features of the prayer meeting that followed the release of Peter and John? How do they compare with encouragements to pray found elsewhere in the New Testament?
Acts 4:23–31, Philippians 4:6–7, 2 Thessalonians 3:1–3, 2 Corinthians 13:7, Hebrews 13:8–21

C. What motivates these new believers to be so selfless, generous and supportive of each other?
Acts 4:32–37, Acts 20:34–35, Hebrews 10:24–25, 1 John 3:11–17

Chapter 11

A double death

Acts 5:1–11

¹ *But a certain man named Ananias, with Sapphira his wife, sold a possession.* ² *And he kept back part of the proceeds, his wife also being aware of it, and brought a certain part and laid it at the apostles' feet.* ³ *But Peter said, 'Ananias, why has Satan filled your heart to lie to the Holy Spirit and keep back part of the price of the land for yourself?* ⁴ *While it remained, was it not your own? And after it was sold, was it not in your own control? Why have you conceived this thing in your heart? You have not lied to men but to God.'*

⁵ *Then Ananias, hearing these words, fell down and breathed his last. So great fear came upon all those who heard these things.* ⁶ *And the young men arose and wrapped him up, carried him out, and buried him.*

⁷ *Now it was about three hours later when his wife came in, not knowing what had happened.* ⁸ *And Peter answered her, 'Tell me whether you sold the land for so much?'*

She said, 'Yes, for so much.'

9 *Then Peter said to her, 'How is it that you have agreed together to test the Spirit of the Lord? Look, the feet of those who have buried your husband* are *at the door, and they will carry you out.'* 10 *Then immediately she fell down at his feet and breathed her last. And the young men came in and found her dead, and carrying* her *out, buried* her *by her husband.* 11 *So great fear came upon all the church and upon all who heard these things.*

Acts 5:1–6
Ananias—the sad pretender

The background facts to the unexpected deaths of Ananias and his wife, Sapphira, are simple. We have seen how some early Christians voluntarily sell their property and put the proceeds of sale in the apostles' hands to distribute to needy people.[1] They are not commanded to do so. They are free to choose to sell or not to sell, and to keep or give away any money received. Acts 4:36–37 mentions Barnabas as someone who decides to sell and give. Christian giving is primarily a personal matter between the giver and his, or her, Lord.

But it is wrong to give a false impression of higher devotion, or greater generosity, to God than is the case. That breaks God's moral law, the Ten Commandments,[2] especially the ninth commandment not to 'bear false witness'.[3] That commandment can be broken by an outright lie, or a slight exaggeration, or by deceiving someone in another way. Do not pretend to be what you know you are not!

Ananias is a sad pretender. Perhaps he and his wife see how impressed people are with Barnabas when the news gets round that he has sold his property to give the money to the apostles to use. Unlike Barnabas, Ananias keeps some sale proceeds for himself. That is acceptable. The choice is his whether to donate none, part or all of the money. What is unacceptable is lying to the Holy Spirit. He pretends to have given all he received. His wife is 'aware of it' and is also led astray. She joins in his attempted deception. This is almost the Garden of Eden in reverse, where the woman, Eve, took and ate the forbidden fruit and offered it to the man, Adam, who also took it and ate.[4]

We are not told how Peter knows Ananias is lying. Since the lie is to the Holy Spirit, we assume that the Holy Spirit lets His apostle know somehow. Maybe Ananias' guilty behaviour gives him away? Perhaps their secret leaked out and Peter heard? The fact is that he has lied in his heart and Peter tells him directly, 'You have not lied to men but to God'.[5] He and Sapphira know they have boasted of giving everything when they have given less.

Ananias falls down dead at Peter's accusation. All who hear what has happened experience 'great fear'. No doubt the Holy Spirit convicts all true Christians of God's requirement that they must be truthful and holy. God is more concerned about the purity of the new Christians' testimony to His saving grace than about the early deaths of two disobedient, but still eternally saved, blood-bought children.[6] God sometimes allows or brings sickness as a chastisement or discipline to bring compromised Christians to repentance. He may even remove the lives of some who spoil and soil their public witness about their changed lives.[7]

Ananias' body is covered up by the young men, carried away, and buried. But what about his wife Sapphira?

Acts 5:7–10
Sapphira's conspiracy to deceive
Three hours later Sapphira comes in, unaware that she is now a widow. Peter first wisely checks that she actually did share in her husband's deception. Then he asks if the land was sold for the price that Ananias had dishonestly stated to him. She confirms that it is so. Another lie! Like dirty flies, lies breed lies.

Peter asks why have they 'agreed together to test the Spirit of the Lord'. This suggests that the Holy Spirit has probably revealed their dishonesty directly to him. He tells her of the timely return of her husband's burial party. She 'immediately' falls down by Peter's feet and dies. The young men now deal with her body as they recently did with Ananias' body. How sad. How unnecessary. How avoidable. How challenging for us.

Acts 5:11
Great fear falls on the people again
After her death, again 'great fear came upon all the church and upon all who heard these things'. God requires His people to walk in the light with transparent honesty. They must be truthful in heart, word and deed before God, before the church leaders, before each other, and before an often critical world.

Many wrongly consider lies as minor sins and so tell them too easily. Revelation 21:8 declares that 'all liars' will be judged. Revelation 21:27 states that 'anything … that … causes a lie'[8] will exclude a person from Heaven. A lie can be caused in many ways, because it is false.[9] God is true and demands truth.

Acts 5:1–11
Concluding comment: what if God worked like that now?

These are uniquely exceptional times in the early church, as the events on the Day of Pentecost showed. The early church's selfless view of possessing 'all things in common' is exceptional, too. Although the principles of generous giving and caring hospitality are permanent the practice here in the early church is not a pattern for all Christians for all time. They are helping persecuted and homeless believers who are destitute and have lost their 'bread earners'. Paul later tells the Christians in Thessalonica to go and work with their own hands to support themselves (rather than receive support) and live honestly. He also instructs Timothy to teach that needed support for widows should be by believing relatives working to support them, wherever possible, rather than asking the church to do so.[10]

Similarly today, happily for us, God does not judge by immediately killing all dishonest people. As far as we know He chooses only Ananias and Sapphira in the early church to die like that. Why them? We do not know. God always has His own good reasons. If God dealt with western Christians in the same way as he deals here with Ananias and Sapphira empty churches and very rich undertakers (or morticians) would result! But sadly, as one of the deceased, I would not witness it! How many Christians would remain if all liars were suddenly taken?

The effect on the world would be amazing too. God's strict judgement leading to death might remind men and women of His far more severe eternal judgement after death.[11] Would not people see the enormity of their guilt for *any* sin against the one and only God of total holiness? Would not some repent, trust Christ and be saved? Strangely, it is God's mercy, longsuffering, and patience which allow men and women the time to turn from sin and trust Christ, and so avoid eternal judgement.[12]

But like Ananias and Sapphira, one day we will breathe our last breath. Also like them, we cannot know when we will die, either. Because life is short, we should ask the Lord Jesus Christ to be our daily Guide through life and the Lord of every detail of our lives from now on. By His strength and with His help, we must live for Him, who is *Lord*.[13]

It is urgent for anyone without personal faith in Christ to turn from wrongdoing and wrong attitudes and trust Him now, while there is still time. God's time to come to Christ is always 'now'. 2 Corinthians 6:2 reminds us that the 'accepted time' and the 'day of salvation' is *now*!

Questions on Chapter 11
A double death—Acts 5:1–11

A. Why is it so important to be open with God, to tell the truth, and not to lie to anyone?
Acts 5:3, Acts 5:9, John 16:13, John 14:6, 1 John 3:21, 2 John 1:3, James 1:18

B. What effect did Ananias and Sapphira have on each other? How could it have been different?
Acts 5:1–2. Acts 5:7–9, 1 Peter 3:7, Ephesians 5:25, 33, Amos 3:3 (see NIV for this verse.)

C. In what ways may fearing God be a good thing? What other words or phrases can be used to describe this godly fear?
Acts 5:5, 11, Psalm 111:10, Proverbs 1:7, Proverbs 8:13, Proverbs 14:27

CHAPTER 12

In prison again! and out again!

ACTS 5:12–32

¹² And through the hands of the apostles many signs and wonders were done among the people. And they were all with one accord in Solomon's Porch. ¹³ Yet none of the rest dared join them, but the people esteemed them highly. ¹⁴ And believers were increasingly added to the Lord, multitudes of both men and women, ¹⁵ so that they brought the sick out into the streets and laid them on beds and couches, that at least the shadow of Peter passing by might fall on some of them. ¹⁶ Also a multitude gathered from the surrounding cities to Jerusalem, bringing sick people and those who were tormented by unclean spirits, and they were all healed.

¹⁷ Then the high priest rose up, and all those who were with him (which is the sect of the Sadducees), and they were filled with indignation, ¹⁸ and laid their hands on the apostles and put them in the common prison. ¹⁹ But at night an angel of the Lord opened the prison doors

and brought them out, and said, 20 "Go, stand in the temple and speak to the people all the words of this life."

21 *And when they heard* that, *they entered the temple early in the morning and taught. But the high priest and those with him came and called the council together, with all the elders of the children of Israel, and sent to the prison to have them brought.*

22 *But when the officers came and did not find them in the prison, they returned and reported,* 23 *saying, 'Indeed we found the prison shut securely, and the guards standing outside before the doors; but when we opened them, we found no one inside!'* 24 *Now when the high priest, the captain of the temple, and the chief priests heard these things, they wondered what the outcome would be.* 25 *So one came and told them, saying, 'Look, the men whom you put in prison are standing in the temple and teaching the people!'*

26 *Then the captain went with the officers and brought them without violence, for they feared the people, lest they should be stoned.* 27 *And when they had brought them, they set* them *before the council. And the high priest asked them,* 28 *saying, 'Did we not strictly command you not to teach in this name? And look, you have filled Jerusalem with your doctrine, and intend to bring this Man's blood on us!'*

29 *But Peter and the* other *apostles answered and said: 'We ought to obey God rather than men.* 30 *The God of our fathers raised up Jesus whom you murdered by hanging on a tree.* 31 *Him God has exalted to His right hand* to be *Prince and Savior, to give repentance to Israel and forgiveness of sins.* 32 *And we are His witnesses to these things, and so also* is *the Holy Spirit whom God has given to those who obey Him'.*

Acts 5:12–16
Signs and wonders
God continues to use the apostles miraculously by their doing 'many signs and wonders'. This influences those gathered in the porch of Solomon's Temple. It builds more credibility for their message of forgiveness and eternal life in Christ. Others, scared of the religious authorities, dare not join them. The people esteem the apostles highly, and 'increasingly' many new believers are 'added to the Lord'. In fact, 'multitudes of both men and women' come to Christ.

God so marks out Peter and the apostles as His messengers at this key time in the church's history that they place sick people so that Peter's shadow will fall on some. Presumably that heals some, or why do they do it? From Jerusalem and around, ill and demon-possessed people gather to the apostles. All who come are healed. This is exceptional and a million miles from the con-tricks of some tele-evangelists and pretended healers of today.

Acts 5:17–21
Arrested by men and released by God
But all this hardens the prejudice and the jealous hearts of the high priest and his Sadducee associates. Clearly, Jesus has risen from the dead. People know it is so. They see that the risen Lord is changing peoples' lives through the Holy Spirit and the preaching of the apostles. So it's back to prison for the apostles—but not for long! In the public jail that night God's angel opens the prison doors—we are not told how[1]—and brings them out. He tells them, 'Go, stand in the temple and speak to the people all the words of this life'. They obey and begin to teach there 'early in the morning'. Think how this will further focus the attention of their hearers on the message they preach!

Acts 5:21–26
Where are our prisoners?

Presumably with pomp and ceremony, 'all the elders of the children of Israel' now congregate with the high priest and the Council to hear these men held in custody. The officers go to fetch the prisoners. There is just one problem. The prisoners have gone! The officers return empty handed! The angel did a great job, when leading out the apostles. The guards never knew they had left. Either the apostles were given exceptional quietness and invisibility, or the guards were put to sleep, or both. The angel certainly needed no keys, which presumably were still on the guards' belts or key chains. No wonder their 'keepers' are now greatly perplexed and fear for their future. Perhaps their lives, as well as their career paths, are in great jeopardy now? Are the men by now miles away, having made good their escape?

Then an unexpected message is delivered. The men are in the temple again, openly 'teaching the people'! Off go the captain and officers to bring them back peacefully. They dare not risk being aggressive because the people may stone them. The general public are very sympathetic to the apostles and their message. One wonders how many more people will be in Heaven because of that extra time of gospel preaching in the temple on this eventful morning.

Acts 5:27–32
Does this sound familiar?

Now, back before the Council, the high priest ignores the well-established but staggering fact that the lame man has been healed. Instead he objects to the apostles' teaching in Jesus' name. How Jesus is hated! But the high priest also unwittingly compliments Peter and the apostles in his opening criticism. He says, 'Did we not strictly command you not to teach in this name? And look, you have filled Jerusalem with your doctrine, and intend to bring this Man's blood on us'. That is music in the apostles' ears. In such a short time they have 'filled Jerusalem' with the news that Christ died for sinners, rose again, and will save those who repent and turn to Him! The high priest is guilty of orchestrating the cruel, unjust and unconstitutional shedding of Jesus' blood. But in another way, the apostles would love to bring Christ's 'blood on' him for his blessing. What joy will be theirs if the high priest himself admits he is wrong, believes in Jesus, and discovers—as they have—that 'the blood of Jesus Christ His [God's] Son cleanses us from all sin'.[2] Sadly, that does not occur. Why do guilty sinners—religious or irreligious—refuse to yield to Jesus?

Can you guess what the apostles' reply is to the high priest? They repeat that they 'ought to obey God rather than men'. He has heard a similar response before![3] They then remind him of four things. First, Jesus is alive from the dead. Second, He died as a result of the direct sin of the high priest and his prejudiced colleagues. Third, Jesus has been exalted, by which they refer both to His resurrection and His ascension to Heaven. Fourth, those who obey God's command to repent and believe in Christ receive the Holy Spirit.

God gives the Council yet another opportunity to own up to their wrongs, do a humbling U-turn, believe in the crucified and living Christ, and know God's pardon and presence by the Holy Spirit in their lives. How will they respond or react? We will see as we consider Acts 5:33–42 in the next chapter. Have you responded personally?

Questions on Chapter 12
In prison again! and out again!—Acts 5:12–32

A. How many acts of God can you find mentioned in this passage?

Acts 5:12–32 (especially verses 12, 16, 19, 30, 31, 32)

B. What facts do the Council ignore to support such biased opposition against preaching in the name of the Lord Jesus Christ? Why do they oppose the apostles?

Acts 5:12–32 (especially verses as in A., above) Acts 5:17, Acts 5:28, Isaiah 53:3

C. How many positive things can you find here about the apostles' witness?

Acts 5:12–32 (especially verses 12, 21, 25, 29–32), Acts 4:18–20, Acts 4:12, 1 Corinthians 2:1–5

Chapter 13

Enter Gamaliel

Acts 5:33–42

33 *When they heard this, they were furious and plotted to kill them.* 34 *Then one in the council stood up, a Pharisee named Gamaliel, a teacher of the law held in respect by all the people, and commanded them to put the apostles outside for a little while.* 35 *And he said to them:* "Men of Israel, take heed to yourselves what you intend to do regarding these men. 36 *For some time ago Theudas rose up, claiming to be somebody. A number of men, about four hundred, joined him. He was slain, and all who obeyed him were scattered and came to nothing.* 37 *After this man, Judas of Galilee rose up in the days of the census, and drew away many people after him. He also perished, and all who obeyed him were dispersed.* 38 *And now I say to you, keep away from these men and let them alone; for if this plan or this work is of men, it will come to nothing;* 39 *but if it is of God, you cannot overthrow it—lest you even be found to fight against God."*

40 *And they agreed with him, and when they had called for the apostles and beaten* them, *they commanded that they should not speak in the name of Jesus, and let them go.* **41** *So they departed from the presence of the council, rejoicing that they were counted worthy to suffer shame for His name.* **42** *And daily in the temple, and in every house, they did not cease teaching and preaching Jesus* as *the Christ.*

Acts 5:33
Intent to kill

A neutral observer at the Council meeting may expect a good example from supposedly sincere, honest and righteous religious leaders. Why, then, are they so enraged, or furious,[1] that they want to kill these men? Their only 'offence' is to preach in the name of Jesus. The truth is that the Council is angry because the apostles have repeated that they will obey God rather than the men on the Council. Also they openly put the blame for the death of Christ squarely on the shoulders of those Jewish religious leaders. Their guilty consciences are smitten. Instead of confessing and forsaking their sin, however, they decide to 'shoot the messengers'. They refuse to 'heed the message.' Their evil actions and attitudes, contrasted with the apostles' enthusiastic boldness for their Lord, leave these false leaders offended by what they hear. The fact that truth is at stake is secondary to them.

Today many are still offended by the message of the cross of Christ.[2] It brands them guilty, Hell-bound sinners who cannot save themselves and desperately need a Saviour. Many humble, but bold, Christians across the world face opposition or persecution for their stance for the good news of Jesus' saving grace. Thousands are put to death rather than compromise or deny their trust in Jesus. Some call them foolish to go that far. Jim Elliot, whose life was snuffed out by the lance of an Auca Indian whom he went to reach with the gospel, insisted that 'He is no fool who gives what he cannot keep to gain what he cannot lose'.[3] If God convicts your heart of sin, please do not delay coming to Him through Christ for forgiveness and a new start with God. You never know how delay may harden your heart and make you capable of terrible things in the future you have never yet imagined.

Acts 5:34–40
An unexpected deliverer

The Sadducees are a strong influence on the Council, balancing the Pharisees' significant influence. Unlike the Sadducees, who believe that 'when you're dead you're done for', the Pharisees believe in supernatural matters such as the resurrection from the dead, angels and miracles. A Pharisee, greatly respected by many, is the aged and experienced law teacher, Gamaliel. He has mentored Saul of Tarsus, who will soon become converted and be known as Paul the apostle.[4] He has the apostles removed as he speaks to all his Council colleagues. He reasons that, if God really is at work through the apostles, the Council may find itself working against God. If God is not at work, it will come to nothing anyhow. He recalls two factions that came to nothing: one was led by a certain Theudas, and the other by Judas the Galilean (not Judas Iscariot, Jesus' betrayer.) Gamaliel stresses that God will either overthrow or establish the apostles depending on whether their teaching is wrong or right. He counsels to leave the apostles alone.

His advice is taken. It gives the Council a way out and helps them *seem* to be fair, and save their public face. Some criticise Gamaliel because he 'sits on the fence' like many who see the truth but fail to investigate it. As a Pharisee, he believes in the resurrection from the dead. As an intelligent objective thinker, he knows there is good evidence that Jesus rose and left the tomb empty. He is believed. The apostles are not killed. God has much work for them yet to do!

Acts 5:40
Beaten by losers

The Council calls in the apostles. Before their release, they are beaten even though no wrong-doing has been established. After being beaten, they are told yet again 'they should not speak in the name of Jesus'. Their Master went this cruel and unfair way Himself[5]. Now, as He predicted, His servants must follow Him. If Christ's way was strewn with thorns Christians cannot always expect a deep pile carpet to walk on.[6]

The Bible says that Jesus is *precious* and that those who believe find Him *precious*.[7] Some guilty, condemned sinners turn to, trust and love our Saviour God. Others continue in sin and hate His name. These religious Council leaders do hate the name of the only One who can save them. That is tragic. They are the losers—now and eternally.

One mark of genuine Christian conversion is to love the name of our Saviour, Jesus. John Newton, a former slave ship's captain, later wrote the hymn, *Amazing Grace* after he trusted Christ. He had been a vile man and a blasphemer. He often linked Jesus' name with oaths and bad language. Yet after his conversion, he penned these words:

> How sweet the name of Jesus sounds
> In a believer's ear.
> It soothes his sorrows, heals his wounds,
> And drives away each fear.

Acts 5:41–42
Rejoicing and witnessing

It is unusual for wrongly arrested, detained and unfairly punished people to rejoice! Those beaten without charge become angry and bitter. Yet the apostles, after their unwarranted beating, leave the 'Council rejoicing that they were counted worthy to suffer shame for His name'. Their bodies are sore and hurt, but their hearts identify with their Lord and Saviour, who bore their sins on the cross so they could be forgiven.

Does their ordeal weaken their resolve to make Christ known? Does the beating knock out from them their will and desire to tell others of a Saviour's love, or the need to urge sinners to receive Him as risen Lord in their hearts? Not at all! They now follow a two-fold strategy.

Their witness is still 'in the Temple', the religious place. The authorities hate that thought, but the people love it. Hate it or love it—they continue to go to the Temple to announce who Jesus is and what He has done.

But the witness is also 'in every house'. They want to reach 'ordinary' people where they are, with that same wonderfully good news! Their agenda includes both 'teaching' and 'preaching'.

Teaching helps to make disciples. Those who come to Christ need to be taught the truths of God. That is why Christians read and study the Bible every day, and hear faithful preachers explain God's word each Lord's Day, and at Bible studies during the week.

Preaching concerns proclaiming the good news that Christ died and, rose again and forgives those who repent and believe in Him. Teaching obviously occurs in biblical preaching, and preaching the Bible's message contains valuable teaching. If you know Christ, you need not only to grow in your understanding of God's word. You should also seek to make known to others that they need Jesus Christ to become their Saviour too.

Someone has said that we need to know Jesus better, and make Him better known. These apostles did both those things, in difficult circumstances, and rejoiced. God's grace can help us to do the same!

Questions on Chapter 13
Enter Gamaliel—Acts 5:33–42

A. If you were writing a report about Gamaliel, what facts would you put in it?
Acts 5:34–40, Acts 22:3, Acts 23:6, Philippians 3:3–6

B. What do you learn here about the importance of the name of Jesus, who is both the eternal Son of God and God the Son?
Acts 5:40–42, Acts 5:27–31, Acts 4:12, Exodus 20:7, Revelation 19:11–13, 16, Hebrews 1:1–12

C. What connection is there between witnessing to Christ and rejoicing in Him?
Acts 5:41–42, Luke 10:20, Acts 8:39, Acts 16:34, 2 Corinthians 7:9–10, Philippians 1:18

CHAPTER 14

A problem solved, the word spread, and opposition stirred

ACTS 6:1–15

¹ Now in those days, when the number of *the disciples was multiplying, there arose a complaint against the Hebrews by the Hellenists, because their widows were neglected in the daily distribution.² Then the twelve summoned the multitude of the disciples and said, 'It is not desirable that we should leave the word of God and serve tables. ³ Therefore, brethren, seek out from among you seven men of good reputation, full of the Holy Spirit and wisdom, whom we may appoint over this business;⁴ but we will give ourselves continually to prayer and to the ministry of the word.'*

⁵ And the saying pleased the whole multitude. And they chose Stephen, a man full of faith and the Holy Spirit, and Philip, Prochorus, Nicanor, Timon, Parmenas, and Nicolas, a proselyte from Antioch,⁶ whom they set before the apostles; and when they had prayed, they laid hands on them.

7 Then the word of God spread, and the number of the disciples multiplied greatly in Jerusalem, and a great many of the priests were obedient to the faith.

8 And Stephen, full of faith and power, did great wonders and signs among the people. 9 Then there arose some from what is called the Synagogue of the Freedmen (Cyrenians, Alexandrians, and those from Cilicia and Asia), disputing with Stephen. 10 And they were not able to resist the wisdom and the Spirit by which he spoke. 11 Then they secretly induced men to say, 'We have heard him speak blasphemous words against Moses and God.' 12 And they stirred up the people, the elders, and the scribes; and they came upon him, seized him, and brought him to the council. 13 They also set up false witnesses who said, 'This man does not cease to speak blasphemous words against this holy place and the law; 14 for we have heard him say that this Jesus of Nazareth will destroy this place and change the customs which Moses delivered to us." 15 And all who sat in the council, looking steadfastly at him, saw his face as the face of an angel.

Acts 6:1–6
Godly government

We now see how godly people in authority solve a real problem. As directed by the apostles, food is distributed daily by the infant church to feed needy widows. Somehow their well-meant distribution benefits the Hebrew widows more than the Hellenists who are Jewish widows of Greek origin, often regarded as 'second class citizens.'

The twelve apostles identify that their own priority calling and role is to teach God's word and pray. They authorise the church to select seven wise Spirit-filled men of good reputation to oversee this sensitive and important operation of feeding the widows. They will serve as business managers. The men chosen include Stephen (whom we meet again in Acts 7 and in the next chapter of this book) and Philip (who features in Acts 8). They all are presented to the twelve, who pray for and with them, and identify with them by laying their hands on them. As we hear no more about this problem, it seems that God blesses the prompt and wise action taken to solve it!

Western Christians may never face the same problem, though in some countries up to ten percent of a congregation may be destitute widows. Here are valuable principles about how to tackle any problem that faces God's people anywhere. First, make sure that Bible teaching and prayer are always top priorities. Then, recognise, face, and tackle any problem honestly, objectively and impartially. Next, if converted, spiritually-minded, able and wise Christians are involved, delegate the problem to them to handle. Give them responsibility with authority over the delegated area. Encourage leaders to identify, pray with, and pray for those dealing with the problem, and keep themselves informed. Many problems would be solved by such prayerfully backed delegation.

Acts 6:7
God's word gives growth

So the apostles can now concentrate on communicating with God in prayer, and sharing God's word with men and women. Unsurprisingly, 'the word of God spread, and the number of the disciples multiplied greatly in Jerusalem'. Disciples are made when God's word is taught by Spirit-filled people who pray and are prayed for. How pleased they must be that 'a great many of the priests' become 'obedient to the faith'. They become disciples too. Those who are saved, obey the Lord who has saved them. As we have received 'Christ Jesus the Lord', so we are commanded to 'walk in Him'.[1] The fact that a 'great many' priests become Christians underlines that religious people, no less than pagan or irreligious folks, need their sin forgiven by personal faith in Christ. Being a priest, pastor, clergyman, leader or Bible teacher does not guarantee being a true Christian. The conversion of John Wesley, already a devout clergyman, demonstrates that! The truth of the best known gospel verse of all, John 3:16, says, 'God so loved the world that He gave His only begotten Son, that *whoever believes in Him* should not perish but have everlasting life'. *Whoever* includes religious people. These priests, who know so much about the Old Testament law, sacrifices and priesthood, now should understand that the last High Priest offered the last sacrifice for sins, when Jesus gave His sinless body on the cross. He died as the Lamb of God to save them.[2]

Acts 6:8–14
Personal persecution

All seems to be going very well. The Hebrew and Hellenist widows are well catered for. The apostles are fulfilling their role with great effect, and many priests are converted. Just as it seems 'everything in the garden is wonderful', here comes persecution! This time it does not start with the corrupt religious Council in Jerusalem, though it will soon fully involve their biased cruelty also.

Stephen is not only a godly business manager helping to feed the widows and to solve the earlier conflict between the two groups of widows. He is also a man 'full of faith and power' who speaks the word of God with authority. God-given wisdom and the working of God's Spirit enable him to speak like this. He is fully identified with the twelve apostles and their message of forgiveness through Christ alone, and so God empowers him to perform 'wonders and signs among the people'. Observers and hearers will know that he really is sharing God's authentic message.

Jews having their roots in Cyrene, Alexandria, Cilicia and Asia[3] come and dispute with him. They soon realise they cannot win their arguments, because of Stephen's God-given wisdom. However, they do not admit they are wrong. That would oblige them to repent from their sins and trust the Lord Jesus Christ. Instead they motivate liars to say they have heard Stephen blaspheming Moses, the writer of the books of the Old Testament law,[4] and God. The people, the elders and the scribes then seize him and bring him to—guess who?—yes, the Council. That is an appropriate arena for any dishonest claims against Christians to be heard by prejudiced Christ-haters, as we have already seen.

For good measure, they secretly arrange for false witnesses to attend. They will feel at home in front of the crooked Council as they will untruthfully claim there that Stephen 'does not cease to speak blasphemous words against this holy place and the law' and that 'Jesus of Nazareth will destroy this place and change the customs which Moses delivered to us'.

Jesus Himself was lied against.[5] Eventually that led to His death at the hand of sinful and wicked men, but sovereignly planned by God in eternity as the only means by which our sins could be paid for.[6] Now we will see the start of the moving account of the death of Jesus' first martyr.

Acts 6:15
The irony of it all
Verse 15 tells us that the Council members gaze at Stephen, now appearing before them. They all see that his face is like 'the face of an angel'. Most of the Council members are Sadducees, who do not even believe in angels! How do they know that Stephen's face is angel-like? How does this exceptional change in the face of a follower of the Lord Jesus Christ affect their existing bias against His name and His followers? These are questions not answered here! But they must notice the big difference between Stephen and others who might be condemned to death for blasphemy. Especially so, when they know the charges are false.

There is a striking double irony. Here is a court which claims to believe in God and yet unjustly denies God's word! In that court are influential people who deny the existence of angels and yet see a man with a face like an angel! The Council members will be even more struck by what they hear soon. Stephen will boldly challenge them in what is supposed to be his defence speech. God is, and will be present with His persecuted follower as he soon will become the first martyr for the Lord Jesus Christ.

Questions on Chapter 14
A Problem Solved, the Word Spread, and Opposition Stirred—Acts 6:1–15

    A. What do you learn from this passage about how godly people can solve real and practical problems? How do the Holy Spirit and God's wisdom help?
       Acts 6:1–6, James 1:5, Galatians 5:22–26

    B. Are you surprised to learn that a great many priests are converted? What do you think would help them to come to Christ, and what would hinder them?

Acts 6:7, Acts 4:1–4, Acts 5:38–39, Proverbs 29:25, Galatians 5:11, Matthew 7:7, Romans 10:13

C. Does the existence of opposition or persecution mean that God is not at work? Say why you answer the way you do. Acts 6:8–15, 1 Corinthians 16:9, 2 Timothy 3:10–13, Acts 8:1–4, Acts 9:5

CHAPTER 15

Stephen's defence before the Council

ACTS 7:1–53

¹ *And the high priest said, 'Are these things so?'*

² *And Stephen said:*

'Brothers and fathers, hear me. The God of glory appeared to our father Abraham when he was in Mesopotamia, before he lived in Haran, ³ *and said to him, "Go out from your land and from your kindred and go into the land that I will show you."* ⁴ *Then he went out from the land of the Chaldeans and lived in Haran. And after his father died, God removed him from there into this land in which you are now living.* ⁵ *Yet he gave him no inheritance in it, not even a foot's length, but promised to give it to him as a possession and to his offspring after him, though he had no child.* ⁶ *And God spoke to this effect—that his offspring would be sojourners in a land belonging to others, who*

would enslave them and afflict them four hundred years. ⁷ "But I will judge the nation that they serve," said God, "and after that they shall come out and worship me in this place." ⁸ And he gave him the covenant of circumcision. And so Abraham became the father of Isaac, and circumcised him on the eighth day, and Isaac became the father of Jacob, and Jacob of the twelve patriarchs.

⁹ And the patriarchs, jealous of Joseph, sold him into Egypt; but God was with him ¹⁰ and rescued him out of all his afflictions and gave him favor and wisdom before Pharaoh, king of Egypt, who made him ruler over Egypt and over all his household. ¹¹ Now there came a famine throughout all Egypt and Canaan, and great affliction, and our fathers could find no food. ¹² But when Jacob heard that there was grain in Egypt, he sent out our fathers on their first visit. ¹³ And on the second visit Joseph made himself known to his brothers, and Joseph's family became known to Pharaoh. ¹⁴ And Joseph sent and summoned Jacob his father and all his kindred, seventy-five persons in all. ¹⁵ And Jacob went down into Egypt, and he died, he and our fathers ¹⁶ and they were carried back to Shechem and laid in the tomb that Abraham had bought for a sum of silver from the sons of Hamor in Shechem.

¹⁷ But as the time of the promise drew near, which God had granted to Abraham, the people increased and multiplied in Egypt ¹⁸ until there arose over Egypt another king who did not know Joseph. ¹⁹ He dealt shrewdly with our race and forced our fathers to expose their infants, so that they would not be kept alive. ²⁰ At this time Moses was born; and he was beautiful in God's sight. And he was brought up for three months in his father's house, ²¹ and when he was exposed, Pharaoh's daughter adopted him and brought him up as her own son. ²² And Moses was instructed in all the wisdom of the Egyptians, and he was mighty in his words and deeds. ²³ When he was forty years old, it came into his heart to visit his brothers, the children of Israel. ²⁴ And seeing one of

them being wronged, he defended the oppressed man and avenged him by striking down the Egyptian. 25 He supposed that his brothers would understand that God was giving them salvation by his hand, but they did not understand. 26 And on the following day he appeared to them as they were quarreling and tried to reconcile them, saying, "Men, you are brothers. Why do you wrong each other?" 27 But the man who was wronging his neighbor thrust him aside, saying, "Who made you a ruler and a judge over us? 28 Do you want to kill me as you killed the Egyptian yesterday?" 29 At this retort Moses fled and became an exile in the land of Midian, where he became the father of two sons.

30 Now when forty years had passed, an angel appeared to him in the wilderness of Mount Sinai, in a flame of fire in a bush. 31 When Moses saw it, he was amazed at the sight, and as he drew near to look, there came the voice of the Lord: 32 "I am the God of your fathers, the God of Abraham and of Isaac and of Jacob." And Moses trembled and did not dare to look. 33 Then the Lord said to him, "Take off the sandals from your feet, for the place where you are standing is holy ground. 34 I have surely seen the affliction of my people who are in Egypt, and have heard their groaning, and I have come down to deliver them. And now come, I will send you to Egypt."

35 This Moses, whom they rejected, saying, "Who made you a ruler and a judge?"—this man God sent as both ruler and redeemer by the hand of the angel who appeared to him in the bush. 36 This man led them out, performing wonders and signs in Egypt and at the Red Sea and in the wilderness for forty years. 37 This is the Moses who said to the Israelites, "God will raise up for you a prophet like me from your brothers." 38 This is the one who was in the congregation in the wilderness with the angel who spoke to him at Mount Sinai, and with our fathers. He received living oracles to give to us. 39 Our fathers refused to obey him, but thrust him aside, and in their hearts they

turned to Egypt, ⁴⁰ saying to Aaron, "Make for us gods who will go before us. As for this Moses who led us out from the land of Egypt, we do not know what has become of him." ⁴¹ And they made a calf in those days, and offered a sacrifice to the idol and were rejoicing in the works of their hands. ⁴² But God turned away and gave them over to worship the host of heaven, as it is written in the book of the prophets: "Did you bring to me slain beasts and sacrifices, during the forty years in the wilderness, O house of Israel? ⁴³ You took up the tent of Moloch and the star of your god Rephan, the images that you made to worship; and I will send you into exile beyond Babylon." ⁴⁴ Our fathers had the tent of witness in the wilderness, just as he who spoke to Moses directed him to make it, according to the pattern that he had seen.

⁴⁵ Our fathers in turn brought it in with Joshua when they dispossessed the nations that God drove out before our fathers. So it was until the days of David, ⁴⁶ who found favor in the sight of God and asked to find a dwelling place for the God of Jacob. ⁴⁷ But it was Solomon who built a house for him. ⁴⁸ Yet the Most High does not dwell in houses made by hands, as the prophet says, ⁴⁹ "Heaven is my throne, and the earth is my footstool. What kind of house will you build for me, says the Lord, or what is the place of my rest? ⁵⁰ Did not my hand make all these things?"

⁵¹ You stiffnecked and uncircumcised in heart and ears! You always resist the Holy Spirit; as your fathers did, so do you. ⁵² Which of the prophets did your fathers not persecute? And they killed those who foretold the coming of the Just One, of whom you now have become the betrayers and murderers, ⁵³ who have received the law by the direction of angels and have not kept it.'

Acts 7:1
The cynical question that need not be asked
Stephen is falsely charged with blasphemy against God and Moses,[1] speaking against the temple and God's law, and predicting that Jesus will destroy the temple and Jewish customs.[2] The chief priest is probably behind the perjurers' wicked lies, supported by his unjust, dishonest and biased Council of 'judges'. Stephen is a God-fearing man of deep integrity and compassion. He neither blasphemed God, nor criticised Moses, nor predicted Jesus' destroying the temple, nor His changing Moses' customs. Perjurers accuse a righteous man of blasphemy! How bizarre and wicked!

Stephen's insistence on God's truth that Jesus is both eternally Divine and sinlessly human[3] is regarded as blasphemy by those who reject Jesus as Messiah and so oppose him too. Jesus was falsely misrepresented when, talking about the temple, he predicted the coming death and resurrection of His own body.[4] He never said He would destroy the temple. So why should his devoted follower, Stephen, claim that He did?

The high priest asks, 'Are these things so?' What seems a reasonable question starts the next hypocritical charade of so-called 'justice.' Jesus earlier met the same deceitful opposition from the same religious rulers, as did Peter and John.[5]

Acts 7:2–53
The defence speech that is so much more than a defence speech!
Like his Saviour before him, Stephen makes no attempt to defend or save himself. He knows that the crooked Council has already reached its verdict and decided its sentence. The case against him will be 'proved'. He will be stoned for blasphemy. He has

a higher and nobler aim than saving his own skin. Like Peter and John, he now bravely takes the opportunity to speak for His Lord. In Acts 7:2–50, he shares God's word with his Jewish hearers through recounting their own history. In Acts 7:51–53, he applies its unpalatable truths to their hard hearts, no doubt hoping that some will repent of their sins and trust in the Saviour Christ, whom they now hate.

Acts 7:2–50
The history lesson that is so much more than a history lesson!

The history of Israel's up and down relationship with their God is riddled with pride, rebellion, hard-heartedness, self-interest, refusal to listen, and disobedience , despite God's unerring faithfulness. He has often commanded them to repent, return to Him, be restored by Him, and so be blessed. Repentance has been intermittent and often short-lived.

Stephen traces some of God's gracious dealings with his sinful people through men of God whom He equipped and used. He starts with the patriarchs, Abraham, Isaac and Jacob. God made promises and a covenant with Abraham. Although old, childless and married to a barren wife, he would become the father of God's covenant people the Jews. Joseph was Jacob's son jealously rejected by his brothers but raised by God to become their saviour in Egypt in a time of great famine. Pharaoh's cruel enslaving of the Israelites, after they settled in Egypt, is the scene for Moses to deliver Israel after God commissioned him at the burning bush. He was saved by Pharaoh's daughter when Jewish baby boys were being killed. He fled from Egypt after rejection by his own people. He returned to lead and save them from slavery. He then contended with the idolatry and rebellion of the same people. God introduced, through him, pure worship in the tabernacle in the wilderness, as Israel journeyed to the Promised Land. After Moses' death, his lieutenant, Joshua, led the Israelites with the tabernacle into that Promised Land. King David later wanted to build a permanent temple, but God did that through his son and successor, Solomon.[6] Stephen concludes this potted history by stressing God's greatness, reminding the many religious hypocrites on the Council, by using some words of the prophet Isaiah,[7] to emphasise that no building and no temple is big enough to contain the Lord God of Heaven!

Each historical leader mentioned underlines the quality and uniqueness of the Lord Jesus Christ, the God-man, who alone is perfect. He is infinitely greater than all the leaders put together. Jesus said about Abraham, 'Before Abraham was I AM'.[8] He showed Himself to be the eternal God in human flesh. Isaac and Jacob benefited from God's promises and covenant with Abraham. God promises on oath that believers in Jesus are saved eternally.[9] Joseph, a godly man, pictured physically what Jesus does spiritually for those He saves. Joseph fed the starving. Jesus is the bread of life.[10] He feeds spiritually those who come to Him. But Joseph was a mere man who lived, died and was buried in a coffin.[11] Jesus, the eternal son of God, lived a sinless life, died a death that saves sinful people still today, and rose again and lives with the power of an endless life![12] His tomb was empty! Moses was a judge and a prince.[13] Jesus is far greater[14] and the ultimate and eternal Judge and King of Kings.[15] 'The law was given by Moses, but grace and truth came through Jesus Christ'.[16] It is solely that grace and truth through the Lord Jesus Christ, the Saviour, which enables repentant sinners to enjoy God's pardon and receive eternal life. It is not available through Moses or trying to keep God's law.[17] Joshua is Hebrew for 'Saviour': he took

God's people into the Promised Land. Jesus, the only Saviour, takes His people into an eternal Heaven.[18] King Solomon, guided and helped by his father, King David, built the temple. Both father and son are long since dead. King Jesus, God the eternal Son, is Creator and Sustainer of all creation[19] and His name is forever worthy of all praise.[20] He is infinitely and eternally greater than any building, including the temple, because He is God! He also did what no other person could do: He bore our sins and took the punishment for them on the cross, rose again, and lives today to enter the lives of all who trust Him.

Acts 7:51–53
The message that results in martyrdom

Every message needs to be applied practically. Although it will cost him his life, Stephen does that now. He accuses the religious chiefs of pride—they are 'stiffnecked'. They have sinful hearts and refuse to listen to God's remedy for their sin—they are 'uncircumcised in heart and ears'. Like their rebellious forefathers, they 'always resist the Holy Spirit of God' as He seeks to convict them of sin and point them to Christ.[21] They have betrayed and murdered the 'Just One', the Lord Jesus Christ. They are privileged to have 'received' God's law but they 'have not kept it'.[22] They know they are guilty as charged. Stephen's message is over. He will soon be stoned to death. But his sacrifice will inspire Christians of all ages everywhere to witness faithfully for Christ. It will bear amazing fruit in the lives of some of his hearers, including Saul, the holder of the clothes of Stephen's killers. Soon the risen Lord Jesus will remind him on the Damascus Road how hard it was for him to kick against his pangs of conscience[23] on his way to faith in Christ.

Questions on Chapter 15
Stephen's Defence before the Council—Acts 7:1–53

A. What can you learn here from the way Stephen uses the history of God's dealings with people about God, His people, and those who oppose God's message? What lessons can you learn?
Acts 7:1–50 and refer to footnote references throughout Chapter 15.

B. Consider Stephen. What are the main things that strike you about him in this hour of great need? Does he ever blaspheme? How can you avoid taking God's name in vain?
Acts 7:1–50, Isaiah 26:3, Philippians 4:6–7, Isaiah 40:31, 2 Timothy 4:2–5, Psalm 46:1, Exodus 20:7

C. In what ways is Jesus so superior to Moses and the Temple? How will those truths comfort Stephen?
Acts 7:17–50, Hebrews 3:1–6, Acts 7:22, Exodus 2:11–15, 2 Timothy 4:1,8, Acts 17:31 Revelation 17:14, Revelation 19:16, John 1:17, Acts 4:1–12, John 6:68, John 10:26–30, 2 Chronicles 6:1–11, John 1:1–3, Hebrews 1:1–2, Revelation 5:11–12, Philippians 2:5–11

Chapter 16

Faithfulness, martyrdom and Saul of Tarsus

Acts 7:54–60

54 *When they heard these things they were cut to the heart, and they gnashed at him with their teeth.* 55 *But he, being full of the Holy Spirit, gazed into heaven and saw the glory of God, and Jesus standing at the right hand of God,* 56 *and said, 'Look! I see the heavens opened and the Son of Man standing at the right hand of God!'*

57 *Then they cried out with a loud voice, stopped their ears, and ran at him with one accord;* 58 *and they cast him out of the city and stoned him. And the witnesses laid down their clothes at the feet of a young man named Saul.*

59 *And they stoned Stephen as he was calling on God and saying, 'Lord Jesus, receive my spirit.'*

60 *Then he knelt down and cried out with a loud voice, 'Lord, do not charge them with this sin.' And when he had said this, he fell asleep.*

Acts 7:54
The Council at the crossroads
Stephen has told the corrupt religious leaders clearly of God's faithfulness and grace to His often wayward and rebellious people, the children of Israel. He has directly and bravely applied to them those lessons from Jewish history. They are now at the crossroads. They have another opportunity to recognise their own sins, to repent, and to turn to the only Saviour of sinners, the Lord Jesus Christ. Will they stop resisting the Holy Spirit as He leads them into the truth about Christ, the truth about themselves, and their need for forgiveness? They have been here before.[1] Sadly it is more difficult to admit and turn from sin after each prior refusal to do so.[2] That is why the Bible says, 'Now is the accepted time; behold, now is the day of salvation and Today, if you will hear His voice, Do not harden your hearts'.[3]

Acts 7: 55–59
Cut to the heart and the call home
Through the Holy Spirit Stephen's accusers are 'cut to the heart'. This phrase is also translated 'pierced to the heart' and 'stung to the heart'.[4] God has hit these sinners with conviction where they need to be hit—in their hearts. But with animal-like reactions they grind their teeth at him. As the murderous predators sinfully close in for the kill, the Holy Spirit fills Stephen. He does not look at his attackers. His gaze is elsewhere. He sees Heaven. He sees God's glory. And he sees 'Jesus standing at the right hand of God'. The Saviour's finished work to redeem sinners on the cross meant that He '*sat down* at the right hand of the throne of

God'.[5] Now Jesus rises to be *standing* to welcome home personally His first martyr. There will be many more. They are still joining Him even today from all over the world.

Is Stephen overcome by fear? Not at all! The Puritans rightly taught that God does not give dying grace to live with, but to die with.[6] Here we see the all-sufficient dying grace which God gives His brave martyr. 'Look! I see the heavens opened and the Son of Man standing at the right hand of God', he exclaims. As death approaches he cannot stop making much of his eternal Lord and Saviour, Jesus Christ, with whom he soon will spend eternity. How encouraging to all who trust in Jesus! When their time inevitably comes to be 'absent from the body' they will be 'present with the Lord' and will 'be with Christ, which is far better'.[7]

As Stephen glorifies His risen and ascended Lord, the murderous religious leaders cry out. They stop their ears, which are already blocked spiritually to the voice of God. They run at him 'with one accord'. They 'cast him out of the city' like rubbish. They stone him. What is his 'crime'? To love, follow, serve, and speak well of Jesus.

Why don't the Roman authorities stop this illegal killing by the mob? We do not know. Even today in some countries where the gospel is not welcomed, nor tolerated, nor widely known, sometimes police can ignore those breaking the law to persecute Christians. Sometimes current anti-Christian trends in morality and legislation, even in our 'civilised west', sadly lead to unjustifiable opposition and bias against law-abiding Christians by some in authority and others with media influence. One day all will answer to God.[8]

Acts 7:58–60
What Saul of Tarsus saw and heard

The crooked witnesses of Stephen's alleged blasphemy now become his self-appointed executioners.[9] Who guards their clothes while they stone him? None other than Saul of Tarsus, at this stage 'a young man'. Jesus will meet him later on the road to Damascus. There He will reveal that 'It is hard for you to kick against the goads'.[10] Could Stephen's death by stoning cause the Holy Spirit to continuously pierce the arch-persecutor's conscience? Could that same conviction of sin bring him to repentance and faith in the Lord Jesus? Paul, the former scourge of Christians, will confess his continuing awareness of his part in killing Stephen, 'Lord, they know that in every synagogue I imprisoned and beat those who believe on You. And when the blood of Your martyr Stephen was shed, I also was standing by consenting to his death, and guarding the clothes of those who were killing him'.[11]

Stephen remains as Christ-centred in his death as he has been in his fruitful life for God. He is still 'calling on God'. He prays 'Lord Jesus, receive my spirit'. His assurance that Jesus is God increases with each dying breath. He knows the 'Lord Jesus' listens to him in Heaven. He is the 'Son of Man', a Biblical title demanding deity. He is also the Son of God and God the Son.[12] When dying on the cross for Stephen's sins, and for our sins, Jesus had 'cried out with a loud voice ... "Father, into Your hands I commit My spirit." Having said that, He breathed His last'.[13] Now Stephen prays a similar prayer to his risen and glorified Saviour. He, too, kneels down and cries out his last prayer on earth 'with a loud voice'. This also echoes Jesus' prayer from the cross, 'Father, forgive them, for they do not know what they do'.[14] Stephen's love for Christ and for the lost—even for his murderers—is unabated. He prays loudly for all to hear, 'Lord, do not charge them with this sin'. How many of his killers, like Saul of Tarsus, will benefit later from his prayer, repent and turn to Christ?

'And when he had said this, he fell asleep'. He wakes up in Heaven where, as we have already seen, he is 'absent from the body and ... present with the Lord' and he is forever 'with Christ, which is far better'.[15] Christ's first martyr is home!

With eternity in mind, if you had the choice (which you have not!) would you rather be persecuted Stephen or one of his cruel persecutors? Who wins in the end? Who loses? Where will Stephen be a billion years from now? Where will they be?

Questions on Chapter 16
Acts 7:54–60 Faithfulness, Martyrdom, and Saul of Tarsus

A. Stephen's frank talk to the Council members about their own sin brings about a strong reaction against him. How does he react to such cruel opposition? Why does he react like this?
Acts 7:51–54, Acts 7:55–56, 2 Timothy 4:1–5, Romans 10:17, Acts 5:29–32, Matthew 10:17–20

B. Why is repentance such an important part of the good news of Jesus Christ? What results from the continuing failure and refusal to repent?
Acts 7:54–59, Acts 2:38–40, Acts 3:19, Acts 5:30–31, Luke 24:46–49, Matthew 3:1–8, Luke 3:1–8, Mark 1:14–15

C. In how many ways do you see God's grace sustaining Stephen as he faces persecution and then martyrdom?
Acts 7:55–56, 59–60, 2 Corinthians 12:9, Romans 8:37–39, Isaiah 40:31, Philippians 4:13

Chapter 17

'The blood of the martyrs is the seed of the Church'

Acts 8:1–8

1 *Now Saul was consenting to his death. At that time a great persecution arose against the church which was at Jerusalem; and they were all scattered throughout the regions of Judea and Samaria, except the apostles.* 2 *And devout men carried Stephen to his burial, and made great lamentation over him.* 3 *As for Saul, he made havoc of the church, entering every house, and dragging off men and women, committing them to prison.* 4 *Therefore those who were scattered went everywhere preaching the word.*

5 *Then Philip went down to the city of Samaria and preached Christ to them.* 6 *And the multitudes with one accord heeded the things spoken by Philip, hearing and seeing the miracles which he did.* 7 *For unclean spirits, crying with a loud voice, came out of many who were possessed;*

and many who were paralyzed and lame were healed. 8 And there was great joy in that city.

Acts 8:1–4
Persecution—helping to carry out the commission of Christ

After His resurrection, Jesus announced His mission statement for His church. In Acts 1:8, He said, 'you shall receive power when the Holy Spirit has come upon you; and you shall be witnesses to Me in Jerusalem, and in all Judea and Samaria, and to the end of the earth'. The preaching of the good news about Jesus Christ 'here, there and everywhere', started 'here' (Jerusalem) and must spread to 'there' (Judea and Samaria), and reach 'everywhere' (the end of the earth).

The Holy Spirit empowers His disciples to live for Jesus, to witness for Him, to serve Him, and even to die for Him. The principle of 'here, there and everywhere' continues worldwide today. People from all nations who have been saved, forgiven, changed, and blessed by trusting Christ urge others to turn from sin and trust in Him too.

In Jerusalem, although many priests are converted, the religious leaders' opposition is cruel, vicious and dishonest. Stephen's martyrdom, consented to and supported by Saul, triggers great persecution 'against the church' *here* at Jerusalem. This scatters believers 'throughout the regions of Judea and Samaria'. These radiant, born-again, Spirit-filled, witnessing, Christians live out and teach God's word. They focus on the gospel of Christ's cross and resurrection. So the good seed is also sown 'there', in the second target area of the church's mission statement. God is in control of circumstances. We will see that 'the blood of the martyrs is the seed of the church'.

Stephen is not forgotten. His body is carried to burial by 'devout men' who identify with him and his Saviour, despite rising persecution. They lament him greatly. Although those trusting Christ rejoice in the home-call to Heaven of loved ones or Christian friends, they understandably mourn their loss. It is not easy for bereaved families, friends, or fellow Christians. When the Lord's followers mourn they know that God is in control and knows best, even when emotions tug them in various directions. He gives grace to help in time of need.[1]

Three factors in this Jerusalem persecution help the church to spread its gospel influence from 'here' to 'there'.

First, the apostles set a brave example by staying in the place of duty and danger, Jerusalem. All are scattered 'except the apostles'. Their two-fold task of giving themselves to prayer and to ministering God's word has not changed.[2] They oversee and help others, including those in danger or with loved ones in prison. A lost world of people must be reached with the gospel, so these brave leaders face persecution and martyrdom, and stay put. It can be right to flee persecution, but never right to flee from duty.

Second, Saul of Tarsus master-minds and leads the cruel persecution. This involves terrible 'havoc', going into 'every house' (no exceptions—all are opposed), 'dragging off of men and women', and committing Christians to 'prison'. Some must think that Saul is a hopeless case and beyond conversion. But others will target his huge anti-Christian profile in their prayers. Christ's followers today should also pray for well-known 'public anti-Christians'. God's saving grace is always needed to bring anyone to faith and forgiveness. No-one can be saved without God's miraculous work in their heart. Saul is no different from modern day opponents and persecutors of Christians. But our

God is the God of miracles for whom nothing is impossible.[3] Saul will finally 'lose' this battle and yet eternally 'gain'.[4] Many will come to Christ through him. Millions through the ages will be blessed through his writing thirteen or fourteen[5] New Testament letters under God the Holy Spirit's influence.

Third, there is an amazing upside! Note the word *therefore* in verse 4. 'Therefore, those who were scattered went everywhere preaching the word'. The persecution of faithful Christians works to spread the good news of Jesus Christ. The 'blood of the martyrs' actually becomes 'the seed of the church.' No committee decides where to target its evangelistic work. Here, truly converted people, who have come to love Christ and flee persecution, simply want other people to know Him too. They cannot stop telling others they meet about Him. Their changed lives show that He really makes a difference. Obviously they would prefer a peaceful life, back home, but that has been taken from them for now. So they do all they can to spread the gospel. When they reach their eternal home with Christ, they will hear their Lord's 'Well done!'[6] By 'preaching the word', the Bible no doubt means that they share Christ crucified with sinners and teach the Bible to Christians. They do what they have seen the apostles do in Jerusalem. Their example still challenges Christians today. Do we share our Saviour, wisely, sensitively, clearly and kindly with others?

Acts 8:5–8
Philip's example, message and results
Samaria, once the capital of Israel's northern kingdom when Jerusalem was the capital of Judah in the south, became apostate and idolatrous. The Assyrians conquered it in 722 BC. This led to Gentiles of varying religious backgrounds moving there and

intermarrying with the Jewish population. A sort of half-nation of people, known as Samaritans, resulted. Jews, especially from Jerusalem and the south, and Samaritans became hostile to each other. That is why Jesus' taught that a 'neighbour' is anyone in need, irrespective of origin or religion, when he told of the 'good Samaritan' who saved and helped a wounded Jew.[7]

Philip leaves Jerusalem to go to Samaria with one aim and one message in mind. He preaches 'Christ to them'. Amazing signs and wonders authenticate his close link with the apostles' God-given message of salvation in Christ alone by personal repentance and faith alone. But he does not focus on those signs and wonders. He preaches *Christ*. Later in the chapter, when he meets the Ethiopian treasurer under Queen Candace, he preaches *Jesus* to him,[8] just as he preaches *Christ* now. There is no other message to preach except Jesus Christ, and Him crucified and risen again! That is why the apostles insist about Jesus Christ that 'Nor is there salvation in any other, for there is no other name under heaven given among men by which we must be saved'.[9] If you are a real Christian, Jesus has saved you! He is the only Saviour who can save anyone. So Christians preach Him.

'Multitudes with one accord' listen to Philip attentively. As he casts out 'unclean spirits' and heals the 'paralyzed and lame', people are convinced that God is at work.

'There was great joy in that city'. Turning from sin to Christ, from death to life, and from Hell to Heaven always brings joy! That is not only so for the person who is saved. It is true too for the person sharing the gospel—and even for the angels in Heaven who rejoice when a single person comes to faith in Jesus![10] 'Salvation is of the LORD!'[11] It is His work. Do you have the joy of knowing Christ? Do you rejoice in sharing Him with others? We will see more of how Philip is involved in this very soon.

Questions on Chapter 17
'the blood of the martyrs is the seed of the church'—
Acts 8:1–8

A. Under God's overall control, what circumstances help to guide the Christians in the Jerusalem church? As guidance is not only a question of how we *feel* about something, what else is important in Christians being guided by God?
Acts 8:1–4, Romans 8:28, Proverbs 3:5–6, Romans 12:1–2, Genesis 50:20, Proverbs 27:1

B. In Acts 9, we will learn about Jesus speaking to Saul of Tarsus. What have you learned about Saul so far before his conversion? How is he like many non-Christians? In what ways is he different to most?
Acts 7:58, Acts 8:1–3, Acts 9:1–2, Philippians 3:2–7

C. Compare the spreading of the gospel through the persecuted and scattered Christians with the way it is spread through Philip's preaching in Samaria. What similarities and differences are there? What good examples do they give us to follow?
Acts 8:4–8, 1 Corinthians 1:23–24, 1 Corinthians 15:3–4 (NIV), 1 Corinthians 2:2, Acts 8:35, Acts 4:12

Chapter 18

Sorcery

Acts 8:9–25

9 *But there was a certain man called Simon, who previously practiced sorcery in the city and astonished the people of Samaria, claiming that he was someone great,* 10 *to whom they all gave heed, from the least to the greatest, saying, 'This man is the great power of God.'* 11 *And they heeded him because he had astonished them with his sorceries for a long time.* 12 *But when they believed Philip as he preached the things concerning the kingdom of God and the name of Jesus Christ, both men and women were baptized.* 13 *Then Simon himself also believed; and when he was baptized he continued with Philip, and was amazed, seeing the miracles and signs which were done.*

14 *Now when the apostles who were at Jerusalem heard that Samaria had received the word of God, they sent Peter and John to them,* 15 *who, when they had come down, prayed for them that they might receive the Holy Spirit.* 16 *For as yet He had fallen upon none of them. They*

had only been baptized in the name of the Lord Jesus. [17] *Then they laid hands on them, and they received the Holy Spirit.*

[18] *And when Simon saw that through the laying on of the apostles' hands the Holy Spirit was given, he offered them money,* [19] *saying, 'Give me this power also, that anyone on whom I lay hands may receive the Holy Spirit.'* [20] *But Peter said to him, 'Your money perish with you, because you thought that the gift of God could be purchased with money!* [21] *You have neither part nor portion in this matter, for your heart is not right in the sight of God.* [22] *Repent therefore of this your wickedness, and pray God if perhaps the thought of your heart may be forgiven you.* [23] *For I see that you are poisoned by bitterness and bound by iniquity.'* [24] *Then Simon answered and said, 'Pray to the Lord for me, that none of the things which you have spoken may come upon me.'*

[25] *So when they had testified and preached the word of the Lord, they returned to Jerusalem, preaching the gospel in many villages of the Samaritans.*

Acts 8:9–13
An amazed magician

Simon the sorcerer, or magician, is a well-known celebrity in Samaria. Samaritans from all backgrounds, 'astonished' by his actions over a long period of time, believe his claim that he is someone great. They even call him 'the great power of God.' Some people believe anything as long as it is not in the Bible! Even some Christians are fooled by extravagant claims of spiritual power and ability made by get-rich-quick speakers, often on TV's 'God channel'.

But the mind of the Samaritan people begins to change when Philip comes to preach 'the things concerning the kingdom of God and the name of Jesus Christ'. How often that name, when applied properly and trusted in personally, brings sinful people into a life-changing experience. Jesus often attracts debate, opposition, and persecution. Here in Samaria, new believers are baptised after trusting Christ for forgiveness and new life.[1] Simon himself believes, is baptised, and continues with Philip, who is an excellent role model for any new Christian to look at. Simon sees the 'miracles and sign's by which God attests Philip's authority to preach His message of salvation through faith in Jesus Christ. He is 'amazed'. This differs greatly from his sorcery that has fooled the Samaritans. God the Holy Spirit is now at work to glorify Jesus and save souls through God's unique message.

Acts 8:14–17
The apostles identify themselves with the Samaritan believers. The Holy Spirit comes.

The brave apostles in Jerusalem hear how Samaria has *'received the word of God'* through the witness of Philip and the scattered believers. They cross historical, racial and prejudicial boundaries to send Peter and John there to identify fully with the new church and believers in Samaria who have received God's word. Until now they have been baptised 'only in the *name* of the Lord Jesus'. His command and commission to the disciples was to 'Go' and to 'make disciples of all the nations, baptizing them in *the name of the Father and of the Son and of the Holy Spirit*'.[2] New geographical ground is broken with the conversion of Samaritans of mixed race. They are accepted as part of God's universal church along with Jews and Gentiles. As with the Jews at Pentecost, it is important that now Samaritans are seen to receive the Holy Spirit and be identified with the existing church and its founding apostles. This is a period of important historical transition as the new church of Christ spreads into other nations. Each new Samaritan Christian has become one of the 'living stones'[3] in their new church. The God-given authority of the apostles' teaching will produce the New Testament. Added to the Old Testament, it will form the final written word of God, as we have it today. The Holy Spirit now comes upon the new members of the Samaritan church. As the apostles identify with these new brothers and sisters in Christ, by laying their hands on them, they receive the Holy Spirit. Every individual who repents and trusts Christ always receives the Holy Spirit personally. The Bible says 'if anyone does not have the Spirit of Christ, he is not His'.[4] No one is recorded here as speaking in different languages, as at Pentecost, but all can tell that Samaria now has a Spirit-filled church under the God-given authority of the apostles and their teaching.

Acts 8:18–24
Where does Simon stand? Is he a Christian or not?

We read in Acts 8:13 that Simon believes and is baptised. But what does he believe? Is he really converted to Christ? Sometimes the Bible gives us puzzling situations to work out from its teaching. In doing that, our understanding of God's word grows. If at times we cannot understand the Bible, our understanding is at fault, not the Bible! Also there are some professing Christians whose life-styles make us wonder if they really are the Lord's. Are you like that?

Now Simon tries to *buy* from the apostles the power to confer the Holy Spirit on people. He has not realised that the apostles lay hands on believers purely to be linked with them and with their new church. Their hands are neither hyper-holy nor mega-magic! They are merely the hands of sinners saved by God's grace.

They have no power of their own. Simon fails to grasp that the Holy Spirit is a Person, not a thing or power to be acquired or dispensed. He is the third Person of the Trinity. As God, He enters sinners who repent. Simon, ignorantly and wrongly, offers money to buy the power he wants. He would see that as another valuable asset in his inventory of magic and sorcery to continue to impress people. Although many say that Simon is 'the great power of God', this is not what a truly saved and Spirit-filled man does! Where is the evidence of true conversion? Is his belief merely nominal and intellectual? In the book of James, the author addresses non-Christians who 'believe that there is one God'. He adds with weighted sarcasm, 'You do well. Even the demons believe—and tremble'![5] To believe only in the mind is not enough. Satan does that too!

Peter tells him to keep his money—it will perish with him. His wicked desire to buy from men what is a gracious, holy and powerful gift of God shows his heart is wrong in God's sight. Peter has no doubt that Simon, despite head belief, is not converted. He has no forgiveness. He is 'poisoned' by his own 'bitterness', probably caused by jealousy that the apostles do through the Holy Spirit what he cannot do by his own efforts. He is 'bound by iniquity', trapped in chains of self-interest. He can have no real blessing, until he is sorted out spiritually. How can that happen? He is told, 'Repent therefore of this wickedness, and pray God if perhaps the thought of your heart may be forgiven you'. Again we see the apostolic message of repentance for sin and the need to put personal faith in God by praying to Him.

Simon is so obviously humbled that it seems he cannot pray for himself. He asks Peter to pray for him, that he will escape the judgement and consequences that his sin deserves. Will he ever repent and be saved? We do not know. We meet people like this. We wish we could push them into the kingdom, but it is up to them to come personally to God, through Jesus, by repentance and faith.

How about you? Do you have faith in God only in your mind, or have you really cast yourself on the Lord Jesus Christ to save you? Have you seen Him dying for you, bearing your sins, and taking your judgement in His sinless, perfect, holy and righteous body on the cross? Have you turned from your wrongdoing to receive Him by faith? Does He now live in your life by the Holy Spirit? Is He your Lord? If not you also need to *Repent* and *pray to God* for forgiveness. Though it is a privilege to have others pray for you, God will hear *you* personally if you come to Him like that. He has promised to hear and answer.[6]

Acts 8:25
On-going sharing of the good news

Peter and John have 'testified' about Christ. They have 'preached the word of the Lord'. They now leave their new Samaritan Christian brothers to grow and witness in that place, so traditionally despised by Jews. They return to face persecution and opposition in Jerusalem. As they go, they are 'preaching the gospel in many villages of the Samaritans'. Remember that the commission to witness to Jesus Christ is to 'Jerusalem, and in all Judea and Samaria, and to the end of the earth'.[7] Samaria now has received the only message of sins forgiven that can reach and save people of any race or religion. And this spreading of the gospel came about by the scattering of persecution, and by the faithful witness of Philip. We will now see him in exciting action again!

Questions on Chapter 18
Sorcery—Acts 8:9–25

A. Summarise Simon's life, desires and spiritual position. What needs to happen to him? How can that happen?
Acts 8:9–13, 18–24

B. What part do the apostles from Jerusalem play in reaching Samaria with the gospel and building up the new church? What general principles of Christian leadership do you see here?
Acts 8:14–17, 19–23, 25, Acts 1:8, Acts 2:42–43

C. Consider the part Philip plays in what happens in Samaria before the apostles come, and compare that with what he does after they arrive. What do you learn about him from that? Is there an example to follow?
Acts 8:4–8, 12–13, 2 Corinthians 4:5, Acts 6:4, Acts 8:14–15

CHAPTER 19

A truly amazing conversion

ACTS 8:26–40[1]

26 *Now an angel of the Lord spoke to Philip, saying, 'Arise and go toward the south along the road which goes down from Jerusalem to Gaza.' This is desert.* 27 *So he arose and went. And behold, a man of Ethiopia, a eunuch of great authority under Candace the queen of the Ethiopians, who had charge of all her treasury, and had come to Jerusalem to worship,* 28 *was returning. And sitting in his chariot, he was reading Isaiah the prophet.* 29 *Then the Spirit said to Philip, 'Go near and overtake this chariot.'* 30 *So Philip ran to him, and heard him reading the prophet Isaiah, and said, 'Do you understand what you are reading?'*

31 *And he said, 'How can I, unless someone guides me?' And he asked Philip to come up and sit with him.* 32 *The place in the Scripture which he read was this: 'He was led as a sheep to the slaughter; And as a lamb before its shearer is silent, So He opened not His mouth.* 33 *In*

His humiliation His justice was taken away, And who will declare His generation? For His life is taken from the earth.' 34 *So the eunuch answered Philip and said, 'I ask you, of whom does the prophet say this, of himself or of some other man?'* 35 *Then Philip opened his mouth, and beginning at this Scripture, preached Jesus to him.* 36 *Now as they went down the road, they came to some water. And the eunuch said, 'See, here is water. What hinders me from being baptized?'*

37 *Then Philip said, 'If you believe with all your heart, you may.' And he answered and said, 'I believe that Jesus Christ is the Son of God.'* 38 *So he commanded the chariot to stand still. And both Philip and the eunuch went down into the water, and he baptized him.* 39 *Now when they came up out of the water, the Spirit of the Lord caught Philip away, so that the eunuch saw him no more; and he went on his way rejoicing.*

40 *But Philip was found at Azotus. And passing through, he preached in all the cities till he came to Caesarea.*

Acts 8:26–30
Get up and go!

After the apostles leave, Philip remains. But in the absence of his leaders he is not idle. God's angel tells him to 'get up and go.' General directions are given first—go 'toward the south along the road which goes down from Jerusalem to Gaza'. More specific instructions follow as he goes towards the 'desert'. He follows those instructions! God's guidance is often like that. He expects us to trust and obey His commands and follow the principles of Scripture. As we do, the detailed path becomes clearer. Anyone who trusts in the Lord and puts Him first in the details of daily living is guided by Him.[2] Guidance is no problem when you stay close to your divine Guide.

'So he arose and went'. Philip is devoted to Christ and to obeying His command to preach the gospel! He sees the chief treasurer of the Ethiopian queen, Candace. Here is a eunuch, converted to Judaism, but not yet to Christ, returning from worship in Jerusalem. He reads and considers God's words through Isaiah, the prophet of redemption as he travels in his chariot, no doubt chauffeur-driven. We rarely find that many people actually are reading the Bible as we seek to witness to them! God's hand and planning is on this situation.

Philip receives his next instruction from the Holy Spirit '*Go near and overtake this chariot*', he is told. He *runs*. He is keen to do God's will and reach people with the good news of Jesus. But this high official is not only converted to Judaism, and not only reading God's word from the prophet of redemption, Isaiah. He also reads the Scripture out loud! As Philip now hears this, he fearlessly seizes his God-given opportunity. 'Do you understand what you are reading?' he asks this influential man.

Acts 8:31–36
It gets better and better and better still!
Amazingly, it gets even better! With humility not often found in lofty status-conscious officials, the Ethiopian replies, 'How can I, unless someone guides me?' Even better still, he asks Philip to sit with him in his chariot. Much better again, the chapter he reads from must be the most cross-centred chapter in the Old Testament. It gives the clearest prophecy about God's redemption through Jesus! It explains, eight hundred years before it happened, why Jesus will die on the cross for us. The situation continues to grow bigger with blessing as Philip continues his witness to this man. The Ethiopian is thinking through the verses he is

reading. He now asks Philip if Isaiah is writing about himself or 'some other man'.

Remember that Philip's passion is to 'preach Christ'.[3] This question is his invitation to preach 'Jesus to him', as He shares about the Lamb of God who was denied justice and who died. Imagine the impact as he explains from the preceding verse, Isaiah 53:6, that 'All we like sheep have gone astray; We have turned, every one, to his own way; And the LORD has laid on Him [Jesus] the iniquity of us all'. Perhaps Philip shares Peter's way of applying this prophecy, as shown in his first letter, that Jesus 'Himself bore our sins in His own body on the tree, that we, having died to sins, might live for righteousness—by whose stripes you were healed'.[4] If so, surely he encourages this treasurer, as Peter encourages his readers, about the Saviour-Shepherd, the Lord Jesus, who forgives them as 'sheep going astray', but rejoices that they 'have now returned to the Shepherd and Overseer of [their] souls'.

The Ethiopian is immediately and deeply struck by his message of Jesus dying for sinners and his need to repent and trust Him. As the chariot continues down the road they come to some water. The eunuch says, 'See, here is water' and then asks, 'What hinders me to be baptised?' Having come from Jerusalem, still buzzing about what happened at and since Pentecost, he has heard of thousands of conversions to Jesus Christ, and perhaps witnessed the baptisms that followed. Now that Philip has explained the gospel to him, the man seems to grasp that, as he has put his faith in Christ, he should be baptised too.

Acts 8:37–39
Believe and be baptised

Philip stresses that baptism means nothing without believing on Christ in his heart. All Jesus has done in bearing our sins and punishment on the cross, and by giving us the power of His indwelling risen life, are not made real to us by any outward ceremony. Neither baptism nor any other ceremony can save us. Only belief in Christ in the heart, with the attitude of repentance from sin, can constitute saving faith. Romans 10:9–11 is helpful here: 'if you confess with your mouth the Lord Jesus and believe in your heart that God has raised Him from the dead, you will be saved. For with the heart one believes unto righteousness, and with the mouth confession is made unto salvation. For the Scripture says, "Whoever believes on Him will not be put to shame."'

If you really have asked Christ into your life to save you, you will be willing to let others know that you have trusted, and do trust, Him. The eunuch's reply shows that he has that saving faith. He recognises that the only Saviour, 'Jesus Christ', alone 'is the Son of God'. He knows Christ has died for him and entered his life. His faith is so real that he now confesses it by word to Philip. Immediately, he will underline that confession in the waters of baptism, even if Philip and his chariot driver are the only witnesses there. (We are not told if there were others.) He is immersed in the water then and there—scorning the dignity of his position—and with Philip he then comes 'up out of the water'.

Acts 8:39–40
On his way rejoicing

How Philip gets to Philistia we have no idea, but we read that he is now there, 'found at Azotus', (also known as Ashdod.) He goes on from there to what is probably his family home in Caesarea. All the way home, like Peter and John who left Samaria before him, he preaches the gospel. 'All the cities' hear of his Lord and Saviour. Philip is serious about proclaiming his Saviour, and so should every Christian be.

After the preacher and the newly converted Ethiopian official part company, we read that 'he went on his way rejoicing'. Does the word 'he' refer to Philip or to the eunuch? The fact is that each of them now goes 'on his way rejoicing'. The good news of Jesus brings joy to those who, like Queen Candace's official, trust Him wholeheartedly. It also rejoices the hearts of those having the privilege of helping others to come to know Jesus as their Lord and Saviour. There is joy in being converted and joy in being used by the Saviour!

Questions on Chapter 19
A truly amazing conversion—Acts 8:26–40

A. What mix of direct instructions from God, guidance by circumstances, and responses by Philip blend together for God to guide him? What can blend together under God to guide you?
Acts 8:26–40, Proverbs 3:5–6, Psalm 23:1–3, John 12:26, Romans 12:1–2, 1 Peter 2:21

B. Consider Philip's conversation with the eunuch. Look at Isaiah 52:13–53:12 and the other references below. If you were asked to 'preach Jesus' from Isaiah 53, what would you say about Him?

Acts 8:30–35, Isaiah 52:13–53:12, 1 Corinthians 2:2, 1 Peter 2:24, 1 Peter 3:18

C. What does Philip do on his way back to Caesarea, and how does that reflect the same approach as other Christians we have met so far in the book of Acts? What example does that give to you?

Acts 8:40, Acts 8:25, Acts 7:51–53, Acts 6:4, Acts 4:31, 19–20, 8–12, Acts 3:12–26, Acts 2:14–40

Chapter 20

The Damascus Road experience— and beyond

Acts 9:1–20

¹ *Then Saul, still breathing threats and murder against the disciples of the Lord, went to the high priest* ² *and asked letters from him to the synagogues of Damascus, so that if he found any who were of the Way, whether men or women, he might bring them bound to Jerusalem.*

³ *As he journeyed he came near Damascus, and suddenly a light shone around him from heaven.* ⁴ *Then he fell to the ground, and heard a voice saying to him, 'Saul, Saul, why are you persecuting Me?'*

⁵ *And he said, 'Who are You, Lord?' Then the Lord said, 'I am Jesus, whom you are persecuting. It is hard for you to kick against the goads.'* ⁶ *So he, trembling and astonished, said, 'Lord, what do You want me to do?' Then the Lord said to him, 'Arise and go into the*

city, and you will be told what you must do.' 7 And the men who journeyed with him stood speechless, hearing a voice but seeing no one.

8 Then Saul arose from the ground, and when his eyes were opened he saw no one. But they led him by the hand and brought him into Damascus.

9 And he was three days without sight, and neither ate nor drank.

10 Now there was a certain disciple at Damascus named Ananias; and to him the Lord said in a vision, 'Ananias.' And he said, 'Here I am, Lord.' 11 So the Lord said to him, 'Arise and go to the street called Straight, and inquire at the house of Judas for one called Saul of Tarsus, for behold, he is praying. 12 And in a vision he has seen a man named Ananias coming in and putting his hand on him, so that he might receive his sight.'

13 Then Ananias answered, 'Lord, I have heard from many about this man, how much harm he has done to Your saints in Jerusalem. 14 And here he has authority from the chief priests to bind all who call on Your name.'

15 But the Lord said to him, 'Go, for he is a chosen vessel of Mine to bear My name before Gentiles, kings, and the children of Israel. 16 For I will show him how many things he must suffer for My name's sake.'

17 And Ananias went his way and entered the house; and laying his hands on him he said, 'Brother Saul, the Lord Jesus, who appeared to you on the road as you came, has sent me that you may receive your sight and be filled with the Holy Spirit.'

18 Immediately there fell from his eyes something like scales, and he received his sight at once; and he arose and was baptized.

19 So when he had received food, he was strengthened. Then Saul spent some days with the disciples at Damascus.

20 Immediately he preached the Christ in the synagogues, that He is the Son of God.

Acts 9:1–9
Saul is stopped

Saul's hates the blossoming Christian church. Armed with written authority from the high priests to the Damascus synagogue leaders, he pursues his murderous threats against Christ's disciples. If found they will be bound and taken back to Jerusalem to face terrible consequences. He is in hot pursuit of them. But God is in hot pursuit of the pursuer! He stops him in his tracks.

Nearing Damascus, a brilliant light flashes around him from Heaven. He falls down. He hears a distinct voice:

'Saul, Saul, why are you persecuting Me?'

'Who are you, Lord?' is his spontaneous question, which the Lord replies to with: 'I am Jesus, whom you are persecuting. It is hard for you to kick against the goads'. Jesus knows that Saul's conscience is being pierced and prodded by the Holy Spirit because of his sinful rebellion against Him and consequent cruelty to His people, just as an ox feels the sharpened point of the goad of its driver forcing it on when it pulls a plough or cart.[1]

Saul is told to go to the city and be told what to do. His travelling companions cannot speak. They hear the voice but see no speaker. They take Saul by the hand as he gets up from the ground, to lead him to Damascus. Saul's eyes are open, but he cannot see. For three days he is without food and drink, and without sight.

Even with healthy physical eyes, Saul cannot 'see' spiritually because his understanding is blinded by his sin.[2] He comes to realise later that his 'understanding' was 'darkened', and that he was 'alienated from the life of God because of ignorance' within him 'because of the blindness of [his] heart'.[3] The same was true of religious Nicodemus when Jesus insisted that he must be 'born again'.[4] Otherwise he would neither 'see' nor 'enter the kingdom of God'.[5] A sinner turning to Christ receives the Holy Spirit, enters God's kingdom, and begins to understand God's word. The result is a growing love for the Bible and a new desire to read and follow it. After his own conversion to Christ, John Newton, the former cruel slave trader wrote 'I once was lost, but now am found: Was blind but now I see'.[6]

Saul, the proud Pharisee and persecutor of Christians opposes the only One who can save him, and give him eternal life and spiritual sight. That Person is the Lord Jesus Christ. Saul now feels deeply his own need.

Acts 9:10–18
Saul is saved
God speaks in a vision by name to Ananias, a Christian disciple in Damascus. His response shows his close walk with Christ: 'Here I am, Lord'. He is available to serve the Lord Jesus. The Lord tells him where to go to find Saul praying. God has also told Saul in a vision that after Ananias comes and puts his hands on him, he will see. Ananias wavers. Instead of going to Judas' house in Straight Street, Damascus he stupidly begins to tell the Almighty what He has 'overlooked!' Does He not know that Saul has been sent by the chief priests to seize and imprison Christians? He tells the Lord of his fear and concern 'for all who call on Your name'.

The Lord simply tells him, 'Go', and reveals His great plans for Saul. The former arch-persecutor will suffer much for the name he once hated. He will carry Jesus' name to Gentiles, kings and Israelites. God makes no mistakes!

Ananias gets the message! His wavering is over. He trusts and obeys his Lord. Off he goes to Judas' house, enters it, and greets Saul as 'Brother'. This warm-hearted Christian welcomes into God's family a new babe in Christ—albeit a special one! Jesus has sent him to bless Saul. As Ananias lays hands on Saul 'something like scales' fall from his open eyes, as God keeps His promise to fill him with the Holy Spirit. Saul is now baptised (presumably by Ananias). His new faith in Christ makes him a child of God and His obedient servant.[7] Washed from his sins, he now gratefully begins a new life of 'calling on the name of the Lord', the Lord Jesus Christ.[8]

There is no other dramatic external evidence to others of his conversion. He does not immediately speak in another language. After all, Ananias and Saul speak the same language. As the apostle Paul, he will later write to the believers in Corinth that 'by one Spirit we were all baptized into one body—whether Jews or Greeks, whether slaves or free—and have all been made to drink into one Spirit'.[9] To others he will stress, if 'anyone does not have the Spirit of Christ he is not His'.[10] Saul clearly belongs to Christ, has His Spirit, and is continually being filled with His Spirit.[11] He is baptised into [meaning 'placed into'] the body of Christ by the same Spirit as every other Christian who is part of the body of Christ, which we call the church. When a sinner trusts Christ for salvation, he receives all this—and a lot more too!

Acts 9:19
Saul is strengthened

Hungry and weak, Saul eats food and is 'strengthened'. Christian love must be practical and hospitable. Here that love strengthens the new brother in Christ, welcomes him into family fellowship, and helps him grow spiritually. Until now, Saul was a stranger to Christian fellowship. Christians were his targets, not his family. Now that changes. His New Testament letters demonstrate his love for his brothers and sisters in Christ. Look at Paul's opening and closing greetings in his letters to see him often expressing this. He now spends time with the Damascus disciples, themselves new Christians. Fellowship, friendship and serving together now fashion his new relationships. A new Christian needs to worship with others on the Lord 's Day, and at other times. He must read and study the Bible and pray personally each day. He will grow and thrill when praying together with other disciples regularly at prayer meetings. Saul now joins with 'the disciples at Damascus'. He will need them, and their fellowship, friendship and support!

Acts 9:20
Saul is serving

The Jews in the synagogues (not just in one synagogue!) at Damascus know Saul has changed! Immediately, like Stephen in Samaria and the apostles, Saul preaches *Christ* wherever he goes. This includes sharing the gospel in the synagogues. The news that he is not persecuting Christians but is preaching Christ will get back quickly to Jerusalem's chief priests. Saul's new life is therefore already on a collision course with his previous colleagues and masters as he brings blessing through the gospel. Just as the scales were taken away from his sightless eyes, they are also removed by the indwelling Holy Spirit from his once sin-darkened mind. He now proclaims to them all that Jesus Christ 'is the Son of God'. His heart is not only made right by God's grace: he seeks to get his understanding of God's word right also. This is essential as he proclaims the truth of God's word and who Jesus Christ is and what He has done for sinners. Jesus is the eternal and spotless Son of God who towers above, yet lives among, dying sinful men. As with Saul, we must make the Lord Jesus Christ the centre of our worship, our walk, our witness, and our work!

Questions on Chapter 20
The Damascus Road experience—and beyond—Acts 9:1–20

A. Describe what happened to Saul on the Damascus Road, as if you were talking to someone who had never heard of it.
Acts 9:1–9, Acts 22:6–16, Acts 26:12–18, 2 Corinthians 5:17, 1 Corinthians 15:8–9, Romans 10:13

B. What kind of man is Ananias? Describe his strengths and any weakness you can see. How important is it to care for other Christians?
Acts 9:10–20, Ephesians 1:15–16, Colossians 1:3–4, Philemon 1:5–7, Hebrews 6:10

C. Consider the words of the Lord Jesus in this passage. What do you learn about the Him and His teaching from these verses?
Acts 9:4–6, Acts 9:10–17, John 10:3, Matthew 28:19–20, Matthew 7:7, Philippians 1:29, Philippians 4:12

Chapter 21

Not so easy for Saul

Acts 9:20–31

²⁰ *Immediately he preached the Christ in the synagogues, that He is the Son of God.* ²¹ *Then all who heard were amazed, and said, 'Is this not he who destroyed those who called on this name in Jerusalem, and has come here for that purpose, so that he might bring them bound to the chief priests?'*

²² *But Saul increased all the more in strength, and confounded the Jews who dwelt in Damascus, proving that this Jesus is the Christ.*

²³ *Now after many days were past, the Jews plotted to kill him.* ²⁴ *But their plot became known to Saul. And they watched the gates day and night, to kill him.*

²⁵ *Then the disciples took him by night and let him down through the wall in a large basket.*

²⁶ *And when Saul had come to Jerusalem, he tried to join the disciples; but they were all afraid of him, and did not believe that he was a disciple.* ²⁷ *But Barnabas took him and brought him to the apostles. And he declared to them how he had seen the Lord on the road, and that He had spoken to him, and how he had preached boldly at Damascus in the name of Jesus.* ²⁸ *So he was with them at Jerusalem, coming in and going out.*

²⁹ *And he spoke boldly in the name of the Lord Jesus and disputed against the Hellenists, but they attempted to kill him.* ³⁰ *When the brethren found out, they brought him down to Caesarea and sent him out to Tarsus.*

³¹ *Then the churches throughout all Judea, Galilee, and Samaria had peace and were edified. And walking in the fear of the Lord and in the comfort of the Holy Spirit, they were multiplied.*

Acts 9:20–22
Saul preaches

Saul immediately preaches Christ whom he proclaims in the synagogues as 'the Son of God'. He staggers his hearers. Can they be listening to the cruel persecutor of those asking Jesus to save them? They think he must be in Damascus to capture Christians, scattered by persecution, to return them to Jerusalem's hostile chief priests.

Saul's powerful preaching extends the influence of the good news of Jesus Christ. His detailed knowledge of the Old Testament is the foundation. He is indwelt by the Holy Spirit, whom Jesus called 'the Spirit of truth'.[12] Jesus promised His apostles, who now include Saul, that when the Spirit comes, 'He will guide you into all truth; for he will not speak on his own authority, but whatever He hears He will speak; and he will tell you things to come'. He added 'He will glorify Me, for He will take of what is Mine and declare it to you'.[13] So Saul confounds 'the Jews who dwell in Damascus, proving that this Jesus is the Christ'.

The Holy Spirit still leads every committed and earnest Christian into God's truth, today, through the Bible. All that is needed is a humble and teachable attitude, backed by prayer, and the disciplined determination to get to know God's word by reading and studying it each day.

Acts 9:23–25
Saul escapes

Death threats, unjust imprisonment, persecution and hardship will mark the life and service of Saul, or Paul as he is called later. He must anticipate what awaits him. He knows how those think who oppose Christ. Until recently he was 'breathing threats and murder against the disciples of the Lord'.[14] He hated anyone trusting in Christ's shed blood and risen life for forgiveness. He detested their insistence on spreading the message that only Jesus can save. The Jews plot to kill him. They keep watch around-the-clock at the city gates for him, in case he tries to leave the city. The governor of Damascus uses a garrison to seek to arrest him, presumably at the Jews' request. The disciples take 'him by night and let him down through the wall' (using a 'window in the wall') in a 'large basket'.[15] Saul flees from persecution and premature death, but never from duty! He is now among those 'scattered' believers in Christ who go 'everywhere proclaiming the word'.[16] The wheel has come full circle: Saul's sacrificial and fruitful service for Christ has just begun.

Acts 9:26–30
That man, Barnabas, again!

So it's back to Jerusalem for the escaped new convert. He now tries to 'join the disciples'. When going to a new city Christians do themselves and others good by seeking out fellowship with other believers. But Saul hits a road block. They are 'all afraid of him'. They do 'not believe' that he now is a 'disciple' of Jesus. It seems too good to be true! How different from his last Jerusalem visit! Do they suspect it is a sly strategy to trap them?

Do you remember Barnabas,[17] the Cypriot Levite who gave the sale proceeds of his land to the apostles in Jerusalem for the needy? This 'son of encouragement' is not only a very generous and self-sacrificing man. He now steps forward to help Saul. He tells the apostles how Saul met Jesus on the Damascus Road, and preached 'boldly at Damascus in the name of Jesus'. Throughout the book of Acts bold preaching for Christ shows the Holy Spirit's work in any Christian.[18] It still does today. Christians, who help new believers to be accepted and integrated into Christian fellowship, do something close to the Lord's heart.

So Saul becomes accepted widely by the church. He moves freely among them. He also witnesses to others with them about Jesus Christ. He makes known the Lord Jesus' name. This leads him to debate with the Hellenists.[19] They make another attempt on Saul's life. His fellow Christians discover that and bring him to Caesarea, before sending him to Tarsus. (I wonder if Philip is also in Caesarea at this time and, if so, whether these two brothers in the gospel have fellowship together there?) In Tarsus, Saul's profile drops for a few years. It seems that during this time he may plant 'some churches around Syria and Cilicia'.[20]

Acts 9:31
Multiplication of churches in peace
We will meet Saul again, in Acts 13. He will start his first of three missionary journeys to the *'everywhere'* section of the Lord Jesus' *'here, there and everywhere'* commission to His disciples in Acts 1:8. Through Peter, the gospel witness will now continue to Judea, the second part of that three part commission to witness to Christ in 'Jerusalem and in all Judea and Samaria, and to the end of the earth'.[21]

Meanwhile 'the churches throughout Judea, Galilee, and Samaria [have] peace and [are] edified'. Saul's conversion and time in Tarsus and on his three coming missionary journeys, takes some pressure off the existing believers. In this time of peace, the preaching of the good news of Jesus and the teaching of God's word continue to blossom.

By God's grace the church increases numerically and in spiritual growth. These Christians do not imitate the world and its loose standards in their worship and service. They are 'walking in the fear of the Lord and in the comfort of the Holy Spirit'. They serve, with reverence, the awesome God in whom they trust. They know the Holy Spirit's help and comfort as He draws alongside them. The Holy Spirit is the Spirit of holiness and a Person of God the Trinity. His comfort is not a response to easy compromises, producing no challenge to live for Christ. It comes from God having first place in their lives as they honour Christ and share His word.

The test of a good and faithful church is not how many attend it. Numerical increase sometimes may be at the expense of faithful teaching of the Bible. Diluted discipleship can attract people for the wrong reasons. So-called 'worship' can be worldly and self-centred, and dishonour God's holiness. We must 'seek first the kingdom of God and his righteousness'.[22] If that results in losing out on numbers, then so be it. But we should constantly seek to reach, win, build up, train, and use as many people as possible in the ways of our Lord Jesus Christ.

So the early Christian population grows in numerical quantity and in spiritual quality. That can only be God's work in them. He is at work in every child of God and will complete that work to His glory![23] But meanwhile there is much for them to do for Him. The rest of the book of Acts is a thrilling testimony to that fact. Perhaps you will join us in the remaining two *Amazing Acts* books to experience that blessing for yourself?[24]

Questions on Chapter 21
Not so easy for Saul—Acts 9:20–31

A. What part do Barnabas and the Christians play in this passage?
Acts 9:25–30, Hebrews 10:25, Romans 12:10, 1 Thessalonians 4:9–10, 1 Peter 3:8, 1 John 4:11–12

B. What do you learn about the witness about the good news of Jesus Christ in these verses? How does boldness feature?
Acts 9:20, 22, 27, 29, Acts 4:13, 29, Acts 9:29, Acts 13:4, Acts 14:3, Acts 18:26, Acts 19:8

C. How does Saul act in the presence of real death threats?
Acts 9:23–25, Acts 9:29–30, Acts 9:15, Acts 8:1–3, Acts 9:1–2, Isaiah 41:10, 2 Corinthians 9:6, Galatians 6:9, 2 Timothy 4:2, 2 Corinthians 6:1–10

A final word

We hope you found blessing and help through the *Amazing Acts—act one* book. If so, please urge others to read it. If you have not taken part in a Discussion Group,[1] or used a Correspondence Course,[2] we hope you will do so and recommend it to others also.

Having an ongoing regular daily time of Bible reading and praying to God is a must for any Christian. You could help to establish that in your life by going through the book of Acts again, and see how much has 'stuck' and what else there is to take in. Follow that by reading the whole New Testament consecutively, and then 'graduating' to the Old Testament and New Testament together. We also hope that you will join us again in *Amazing Acts—act two* and in *Amazing Acts—act three*, both of which are similar to *Amazing Acts—act one* in style and length.

A book that could help you tremendously is *The Bible Panorama*.[3] It walks you through the whole Bible, giving a brief overview of each book in the Bible before covering all the verses in each chapter of each book in sensible clusters very simply and easily to follow. Part 2 explains what the Bible is, how it can be studied, why it can be trusted completely, why the so-called contradictions are not really contradictions at all, how to get the most out of the Bible, how the contents of the Bible were decided, what is the Bible's central message, and why we should read it right through. It contains useful schemes to help you read through the Bible, either in a year, or at your own pace (quicker or slower!) *The Bible Panorama* comes with a CD ROM so you can put its text on your computer.

The prayer of all who have worked to produce this *Amazing Acts—act one* is that people of all ages and backgrounds will come to know Jesus Christ and become His disciples in the fellowship of His church. If you need help or advice please contact whoever helped you to embark on *Amazing Acts—act one*, or write to the author at the publisher's address.

Like the early church, notwithstanding a hostile climate and many difficulties, may we come to know Jesus and make Him known, and embark on getting to know Him better and making Him better known.

APPENDIX ONE

How to run *Amazing Acts—Act One* discussion groups

This Appendix One is to help you organise, lead, promote or participate in an *Amazing Acts*—act one Discussion Group.

At the end of each of the 21 chapters of *Amazing Acts*—act one are three set questions (Questions A, B and C) for your further personal consideration. Each question contains additional Bible references to help. Those three set questions are also the basis of the Discussion Group (and also of the *Amazing Acts*—act one Advanced Correspondence Course—see *Appendix Two,* below.)

Although the 21 chapters together cover all of Acts 1:1 to 9:31, each chapter of the book is also complete in itself. Even if he or she has missed earlier chapters, a newcomer to the Discussion Group will be able to understand any chapter, and find it helpful and enjoyable.

The Discussion Group can run consecutively for 21 weeks. It can just as easily be split up into smaller clusters of Sessions, with a break between the clusters. The clusters can consist of as many or as few Sessions as you like.

To run an *Amazing Acts—act one* Discussion Group, you need the following:-
1. Someone to run it regularly who will spend time to go over the course carefully before teaching it.
2. Somewhere nice and accessible to run it.
3. People recruited to join in it, either few or many. (You can even run it as one-on-one sessions.)
4. A Bible for each person participating, to look up the Bible references in the footnotes and in the questions.
5. A copy of the *Amazing Acts—act one* book to be provided to each person participating.
6. A CD player, in order to play to the group the *Amazing Acts—act one* CD covering the chapter studied.
7. Pens or pencils and some paper to encourage those present to make notes. This is not essential, but will help.
8. An ongoing list of participants and where you can contact them if you need to.
9. Sticky label badges and a felt-tip pen. Make it easy for everyone to know the name of the others in the group.
10. *Amazing Acts—act one Standard* Correspondence Courses to recommend and, hopefully, to give to your group members.

Helpful hints on how to run *Amazing Acts—act one* Discussion Group Sessions:-
1. If it would work well, why not sit people in an informal circle?

Appendix 1: How to run Amazing Acts—Act One discussion groups 167

2. Warmly welcome everyone. Encourage them to take part, without pressing them to do what they prefer not to do.
3. Begin by praying that everyone there will understand, enjoy and be helped by the discussion together.
4. Explain that the book of Acts covers the birth, growth, mission and service of the early church, despite persecution.
5. After playing the complete chapter on the CD, ask volunteers to read twice again the chapter's Acts Bible reading.
6. Check that everyone in the group understands the main points of the passage and the explanation given.
7. Discuss together each set questions (A, B and C), using also the Bible references in the footnotes and questions.
8. Ensure that no-one monopolises the discussion.
9. Do not 'milk dry' each question. Move to the next when appropriate. Dwell on a question if it is helpful to do so.
10. Avoid and reject irrelevant questions unless those questions really merit discussion. Keep quiet but firm control.
11. Before ending the discussion, summarise and apply the points learned. Help any wanting to trust Christ to do so.
12. Close in prayer, or ask someone else to do so. Sometimes a time of group open prayer together seems right
13. Urge the group to review the chapter discussed before the next Discussion Group and to read/listen to the next one.

Appendix Two

Amazing Acts—act one correspondence courses

There are two *Amazing Acts—act one* Correspondence Courses. One is the *Standard* Correspondence Course. The other is the *Advanced* Correspondence Course. When you complete the first successfully you will receive the *Amazing Acts—act one* Correspondence Course *Standard* Certificate. You will receive the *Advanced* Certificate if you successfully complete both levels. You can send in the answers to both the *Standard* Correspondence Course and the *Advanced* Correspondence Course at the same time.

The *Amazing Acts—act one* Standard Correspondence Course
There is a separate Correspondence Course book covering the *Standard* Correspondence Course, which describes exactly what you need to do to complete that course.

How to receive the *Amazing Acts—act one* Standard Correspondence Course
- Ask for one from the person who gave you the *Amazing Acts—act one* book—or
- Order it from the publisher—or
- Order it from a bookshop—or
- Order it from CPR Ministries at the email address admin@cprministries.org.uk

The *Amazing Acts—act one* Advanced Correspondence Course

To gain the *Advanced* Certificate, *first* you need to have completed the *Standard* Correspondence Course. Then complete the *Amazing Acts—act one Advanced* Correspondence Course. All you need is this copy of this *Amazing Acts—act one* book, a copy of the *Standard* Correspondence Course, and a Bible. Then choose one of the advanced three questions A, B, or C, found at the end of each chapter of *this Amazing Acts—act one* book. You should answer in writing on a *separate sheet of paper*.

Each *Advanced* written answer needs to be no less than 150 words and not more than 300 words. It must be written in proper sentences and properly answer whichever of the three questions you have chosen. Please then send your *Advanced* answers to the address stated at the top of each page in the *Standard* Correspondence Course, namely:—

CPR Ministries,
PO Box 61685,
London, SE9 9BL

Some details given in the *Standard* Correspondence Course book will also help you to complete the *Advanced* course.

Here is an example of an acceptable answer to an *Advanced* question: it answers Question B of Chapter 19:—

B. *Consider Philip's conversation with the eunuch. Look at Isaiah 52:13–53:12 and the other references below. If you were asked to 'preach Jesus' from Isaiah 53, what would you say about Him? Acts 8:30–35, Isaiah 52:13–53:12, 1 Corinthians 2:2, 1 Peter 2:24, 1 Peter 3:18*

The message that the high ranking Ethiopian eunuch needed to hear, as a religious man converted to Judaism (which is why he had been worshipping in Jerusalem and was reading from Isaiah, the Old Testament prophet), is the message that every sinful person needs. Isaiah 52:13 to 53:12 is the passage that he was reading in his chariot and from which Philip preached about Jesus. It tells us things about Jesus and looked forward to His death on the cross:—He would deal wisely and be lifted high; His face was 'marred' (or disfigured); He was not regarded as attractive to those opposing Him and they despised and rejected Him; He was the Man of sorrows who bore our griefs, our sorrows, our sins, and God's punishment for our sins, which caused God the Father to smite Him for us; He has bought us peace and spiritual healing through this; He has been bruised for us as our sin bearer because we have gone astray; He saves many people and intercedes for us; and He is worthy of my very highest esteem, whatever His enemies may say, think or do. Like the Ethiopian eunuch I need to believe in Him with all my heart and obey Him, as the eunuch did by being baptised.

How to complete the *Amazing Acts—act one* Standard Correspondence Course

- Decide on how many *Amazing Acts—act one* Correspondence Course Papers you plan to do each week, and be disciplined

to keep to your plan consistently. It is better to complete thoroughly just one Paper each week, and learn from it than to complete several in one week and none in the next. Remember that when you have completed your papers you must send them to the return address stated above.
- Begin by completing the first *two* Papers. The marker of your Papers will then give you useful tips to improve your work. After you have received answers to Papers 1 and 2, send in papers 3–12 to be marked and returned to you, and then finally send in Papers 13–21.
- *The goal of the Correspondence Course studies is to help you to get to know the God of the Bible personally and better day by day. So, don't rush it! Think through the answers and pray about what you have learned. Let its lessons change your life as you trust in and depend on the Lord Jesus Christ.*
- It will, of course, help anyone to learn what Christianity really is, and how the church came into being and grew. But it will be of limited value if your only reason to complete it is to gain a Certificate. However if you allow the Word of God, the Bible to fashion and shape your life each day you will get to know the God of the Bible and know Him better each day! Study His word and apply it to your life. Pray it through. Trust the Holy Spirit of God to help you make any changes in your life that need to be made.
- *After using the CHECK LIST below, please address carefully and send your Papers to the return address stated above.*

Check List

1. Do you have a stamped addressed envelope ready to send? Your chaplain, pastor or leader of your group or fellowship may be willing to send it for you!

Appendix 1: How to run Amazing Acts—Act One discussion groups

2. Is this your FIRST time to send off your completed Papers? If so, include ONLY Papers 1 & 2.
3. When you have received answers for Papers 1 and 2, send in Papers 3–12 and then Papers 13–21. You then will have completed the Correspondence Course.
4. If possible, please complete your answers in black biro or in black ink
5. PRINT your name and address at the top of the Paper. Indicate 'Dr', 'Mr', 'Mrs', 'Miss', 'Ms' or whatever title is appropriate. If you are a Member of HM forces or resident at HM Prisons you MUST include your ID number and location as well as other details (otherwise marked Papers will not reach you). Sadly, even excellently completed Papers without a name or address or ID number have remained in the marker's office.
6. Have you printed or written CLEARLY your answers to questions needing a written reply?
7. Answer *Amazing Acts—act one* multiple choice questions in the Correspondence Course to gain a *Standard* Certificate by placing a TICK IN THE BOX (or boxes if more than one answer is requested) indicating the choice (or choices) you are making.
8. Remember that when you complete and send in your *Amazing Acts—act one Standard* Correspondence Course to a satisfactory level you will receive a *Standard* Certificate.
9. To also receive the *Advanced* Certificate you must FIRST complete successfully EACH *Standard* Certificate Paper AND ALSO complete ONE (ONLY) of the three corresponding *Advanced* Certificate choices of questions which are found at the end of each chapter and marked A, B and C.
10. Write or print between 150 (ONE HUNDRED AND FIFTY) and 300 (THREE HUNDRED) words to answer an *Advanced* Certificate

question. Your answer must be full enough to demonstrate that you clearly understand the question.
11. Have you enclosed a note to your marker if you have any questions or points that need clarifying?
12. Do not wait to receive back your marked papers before you continue your studies in *Amazing Acts—act one*. But do be prepared adjust your answers from your marker's comments. For instance, the marker may suggest you give more Bible references, or may point out a mistake in your thinking. You could then place the requested Bible references in the margin, or make any necessary correction. You will NOT lose marks for inserting the references or making corrections to your work. However, please make any changes or additions as clearly as possible. If it helps you, add another sheet explaining the corrections or additions. Remember that people are praying that you will be blessed and helped through this *Amazing Acts—act one* Correspondence Course!

IMPORTANT NOTES

1. In Great Britain, the return address is printed at the top of each *Standard* Paper. However, a church leader, chaplain, or other group or organisation leader may arrange to collect and forward your completed Papers to that address, or alternatively have your Papers marked by a more local marker who has received our basic marking training and so is authorised by us to mark your Papers. *Standard* and *Advanced* Certificates will only be issued to those whose Papers have been marked by authorised markers.
2. Where Papers are completed outside Great Britain, alternative arrangements will be sought for an alternative return address from which they will be marked and returned.

3. To discuss either of the above options (1.) or (2.), please write to the stated return address, clearly labelling the envelope on the top left hand side *'Amazing Acts—act one Correspondence Course Co-ordinator.'*

Endnotes

Foreword by Chris
1. Gerard Chrispin, *Mark Time* (DayOne, 2011).
2. The author knows 'Chris' personally and well. At the time of writing this it is about a year since he trusted Christ as his Saviour. For prison security reasons neither his proper name nor his location can be divulged. He is currently serving time in the UK for a serious crime.

Chapter 1
1. Luke 1:3. Luke's gospel is the longest of the four gospels, Matthew, Mark, Luke and John.
2. See the opening chapter of *The Resurrection—the unopened gift* published by DayOne, which shows simply but in detail why we know Christ really rose again from the dead.
3. 2 Timothy 3:14–17
4. The word 'baptize' in the Greek literally means to immerse or plant.
5. Mark 1:2–8. See page 13, Chapter 1, *Mark Time*, published by DayOne, or http://marktime.info/read and listen to chapter 1
6. 1 Corinthians 12:12–13
7. John 16:7–11, Romans 1:18, Hebrews 9:27, Matthew 25:46
8. 1 Peter 2:24, 1 Peter 3:18, Isaiah 53:4–6
9. Matthew 24:30, Luke 21:27
10. 2 Thessalonians 1:6–10
11. Acts 1:15–26 shows that Judas Iscariot has died. (See Chapter 2 of this book). So the apostles are down to eleven from twelve. The eleven apostles are: Peter, John, James and Andrew, Philip and Thomas, Bartholomew and Matthew, James son of Alphaeus, Simon the Zealot, and Judas son of James.

12. Mark 3:20–21, Mark 3:31–32, John 7:1–5. But note that not only did some (if not all) of his half-brothers become born again, but that two of them wrote New Testament letters that bore their names. They were James and Jude. James eye-witnessed the risen Christ and presided over the apostles' leadership meetings: Mark 6:3, Matthew 13:55, 1 Corinthians 15:7, Galatians 1:19, Acts 15:13–22. Jude stated he was James' brother: Jude 1:1.

Chapter 2
1. Mark 14:72
2. Mark 14:27–31
3. Mark 14:66–72
4. Luke 22:60–62
5. Luke 24:12, Luke 33,36; John 20:19–20, 26; John 21:1–23
6. Acts 1:9–11, Luke 24:50–53, Mark 16:19
7. Acts 2:1–26
8. 1 Peter 3:18
9. See what is meant by 'apostle' below in Acts 1:20–22, *Finding a replacement*.
10. Psalm 109:8
11. Matthew 26:47–56, John 18:1–8
12. Matthew 26:47–54
13. Remorse is being sorry for yourself. Repentance is being so sorry for your sin that you turn from it to Christ as Lord.
14. Matthew 26:15, Matthew 27:3–10
15. Matthew 27:5, Acts 1:18
16. John 17:12. NKJV translates *the son of perdition* where the NIV uses *doomed to destruction*.
17. Jesus' first recorded message in Mark 1:14–15 included the words *Repent and believe in the gospel*.
18. Psalms 69:25 and Psalms 109:8
19. Only the Holy Spirit can have shown Peter that the Psalms quoted in Acts 1:20 referred to Judas: '*Let his dwelling place be desolate; and let no one live in it,*' and '*Let another take his office*'.
20. Given that God chose Paul as the replacement apostle later, you could argue that Peter was impetuous and the apostles were not careful enough in replacing Judas with Matthias at this time.
21. 2 Peter 1:20–21
22. *Collins English Dictionary* defines the word *lot* as *any object, such as a straw or piece of paper, drawn from others at random to make a selection or choice*.
23. You could argue that a third option could have been to appoint no-one yet. The way would have then been left open for Paul.
24. Proverbs 3:5- 6, Romans 12: 1–2.

Chapter 3
1. Acts 1:13–15

Endnotes 179

2. Exodus 23:16, Exodus 34:22, Leviticus 23:15–22
3. Luke 24:49, Romans 8:9–16,1 Corinthians12:12–13, 2 Corinthians 5:5, Ephesians 1:13–14
4. 1 Peter 2:5
5. God can send fire down and has done so. When He does that, the Bible clearly says so. See, for example, Leviticus 9:24 (the start of the priesthood under Moses and Aaron), 1 Kings 18:30–39 (Elijah and the prophets of Baal), and 2 Chronicles 7:1–3 (after Solomon dedicates the Temple).
6. Luke 24:49
7. Acts 17:30
8. Acts 11:1, Acts 14:27
9. *The MacArthur Study Bible*, Word Bibles, 1997 page 1635.
10. As we will see, the day of Pentecost is truly unique. Other instances of the Holy Spirit 'breaking new ground' for the gospel have certain similarities, but this is different for a number of reasons, including having so many people from different nationalities having God's word preached to them in one place, each in their own language. It broke entirely new ground.
11. The explanation given here in Acts 2:6–7 is that foreign languages are being spoken.
12. See Acts 2:36–41
13. Matthew 7:7
14. Proverbs 14:9

Chapter 4

1. The *IVP Bible Background Commentary—New Testament* by Craig S. Keener: publisher IVP Academic. See 1 Thessalonians 5:7.
2. Read again in Chapter 3, the comments on Acts 2:13 headed *Scrambled thinking: when unbelief defies logic.*
3. Acts 2:17–21 quoting from Joel 2:28–32
4. 2 Peter 1:21, 2 Timothy 3:16
5. The verses below show how Peter now preaches to the crowd about Jesus Christ: His humanity—v. 22–23, His miracles—v. 22, His divinely planned death on the cross through wicked men—v. 23,36, His well attested resurrection—v. 24,32,36, His fulfilling of prophecy—v. 25–36, His ascension to Heaven—v. 33–35, the Father's pouring out the Spirit for Him, His position as Lord and Christ (Messiah)—v. 36
6. John 3:3,7, 1 Peter 1:17–23 especially verse 23
7. R. C. Sproul in *The Reformation Study Bible*, page 767.
8. Hebrews 6:20, 7:1–3,15–16,24–25, 2 Peter 1:11
9. Luke 24:50–53, John 20:17, Acts1:1–2,9 Ephesians 4:8–10
10. Acts 5:31, 7:55–56, Romans 8:34, Ephesians 1:20, Colossians 3:1, Hebrews 1:3,13, Hebrews 8:1, Hebrews 10:12, Hebrews 12:2, 1 Peter 3:22,
11. Psalm 132:11
12. 1 Timothy 6:13–16, Revelation 17:14, Revelation 19:16
13. Romans 6:23, Hebrews 2:3, Hebrews 12:25

Chapter 5
1. In John 14:17, John 15:26 and John 16:13 Jesus refers to the Holy Spirit as *the Spirit of truth*.
2. See what Jesus says in John 16:8–11
3. Romans 3:23
4. 2 Corinthians 5:14–15
5. Romans 10:12–13, Joel 2:32
6. Isaiah 59:2
7. Ephesians 2:13
8. Hebrews 7:25
9. 1 Corinthians 15:1–4
10. This will not always be possible, but often is. For example if I have stolen I should restore what I have wrongly gained.
11. Romans 14:9
12. Luke 23:39–43
13. 1 Corinthians 1:14–17
14. 1 Corinthians 9:16–23
15. Romans 6:1–4
16. Romans 6:5–10
17. Romans 6:4
18. Galatians 2:20
19. John 1:12, Colossians 2:6
20. See chapter 4 of this book, footnote 56, for references to *born again*
21. John 3:3, 3:7, 1 Peter 1:23
22. Romans 8:9
23. 2 Corinthians 5:17, Galatians 6:15
24. 1 Peter 2:2, 2 Peter 3:18
25. Ephesians 5:18
26. Ephesians 4:30
27. 2 Corinthians 1:22, Ephesians 1:13, Ephesians 4:30
28. Philippians 1:6

Chapter 6
1. Paul's greeting the church in Philippians 1:1 gives a clear potted view of the New Testament church structure. There were *saints in Christ Jesus* (= 'ordinary' Christians), *overseers* (also called *elders* or *bishops* simply meaning *overseers*) and *deacons* (or *servants* to whom were delegated special areas of practical responsibility in the church.) For church leaders' qualifications—whether called elders or bishops or overseers—see 1 Timothy 3:1–7, Titus 1:5–9.
2. Ephesians 2:20, 1 Peter 2:4–7.
3. 1 Peter 2:2
4. For a brief but clear explanation of this see chapter 6 of Part Two of *The Bible Panorama*, published by DayOne. Like Jesus, the apostles accepted, believed and taught that all the Old Testament is the foundational part of God's written word. The New Testament forms the second part, in which Jesus' authoritative teaching

Endnotes 181

is recorded in Matthew, Mark, Luke and John's gospels. The apostles were given God's authority to complete His word in the New Testament. See John 16:12–15, Luke 24:13–49, 2 Peter 1:12–21, 2 Timothy 2:14–15 and Ephesians 2:20. Peter shows that Paul's writings are on a par with *the other Scriptures*. 2 Peter 3:15–16. God-given special signs and wonders demonstrate the apostles' authority as His chosen channels through whom God reveals the rest of His message and word in the New Testament. 2 Corinthians 12:12.

5. Acts 17:11
6. Revelation 21:1
7. DayOne's book *MarkTime*, complete with 4 CDs, is a good help to study Mark's gospel. Go to http://marktime.info
8. Hebrews 10:24–25
9. John 1:12, Colossians 2:6
10. 1 John 3:1, Philemon 1:3
11. Galatians 3:28
12. 1 Corinthians 11:17–34
13. 1 Corinthians 5:7
14. 1 Corinthians 11:26
15. Philippians 4:6–7
16. Other translations of this phrase are: *Everyone was filled with awe!* (NIV); *And awe came upon every soul* (ESV); *Everyone kept feeling a sense of awe!* (NASB).
17. 2 Corinthians 12:12
18. John 16:12–15—see also footnote 96.
19. Acts 2:44
20. Acts 2:45
21. Acts 2:46
22. Acts 2:47

Chapter 7

1. 2 Corinthians 12:12, Luke 10:9
2. The ninth hour in Jerusalem then was three hours after mid-day (3.00pm). This was one of the three Jewish times of prayer. The other two prayer times were the third hour (9.00 am) and the sixth hour (mid-day, i.e. 12 noon).
3. *Money or food given to poor people* are called *alms*, according to *The Oxford Dictionary*.
4. Luke 23:44–46
5. 1 Peter 2:24, 1 Peter 3:18, Hebrews 10:19
6. Matthew 1:21
7. Luke 24:13–15
8. Colossians 2:6
9. 1 Peter 1:8
10. John 3:3, 7
11. 2 Corinthians 5:17
12. Ephesians 2:8–9
13. John 3:16

Chapter 8
1. Acts 8 26–35
2. See, for example, quotes in Matthew 8:17, Mark 15:28, Luke 22:37, John 12:38, Romans 10:16, 1 Peter 2:21–25, and also see Mark 9:12, Romans 4:25, 1 Corinthians 15:3, 2 Corinthians 5:21, 1 Peter 1:19, and 1 John 3:5. These are all quoted in the *MacArthur Study Bible* page 1037.
3. Psalm 22 is estimated as written 700 years before crucifixion was practised by the Romans, and Isaiah 53 as 1,000 years, bearing in mind that David's last words are estimated as given in 971 BC.
4. Isaiah 52:13, second half.
5. Hebrews 1:1–2
6. Outside the scope of this chapter, Jesus is God incarnate, our 'Emmanuel', and also God's ultimate and final Prophet, Priest, and King. See *The Bible Panorama*, published by DayOne, Part Two, Chapter 7, page 630.
7. See Romans 3:23, Hebrews 9:27, 2 Corinthians 5:14–15, John 5:24
8. 1 Timothy 2:5–6
9. 2 Peter 3:9, Matthew 11:28

Chapter 9
1. Mark 15:9–14
2. They were annihilationist.
3. Mark 13:9–11
4. They are in a completely new situation and they need God's help through His Spirit right now! He also helps us today!
5. 1 Corinthians 15:3–4
6. John 14:5–6
7. Romans 10:13, John 14:6

Chapter 10
1. Matthew 27:50–54, Mark 15:37–39
2. See the first chapter of DayOne's book *The Resurrection—the unopened gift* to consider this evidence.
3. Proverbs 18:24
4. The Bible speaks about Peter's anticipated death in John 21:18–19. Tradition is that Nero's persecution of Christians claimed Peter's life around AD 67. The unproven tradition is that he chose to be crucified upside down because he did not think he was worthy to be crucified head up, as Jesus had been. John was exiled to the Greek Isle of Patmos from where he wrote the book of Revelation.
5. John 14:6
6. Psalm 2:1–2
7. Levites, from the tribe of Levi, helped in the Old Testament period to maintain and transport the tabernacle. They were not priests (descendants of Aaron). Levites were consecrated to God to look after the sacrifices and material upkeep of the tabernacle and later of the temple.

Endnotes

8. Acts 20:35 and Matthew 10:8
9. Romans 6:23

Chapter 11
1. Acts 4:32–37
2. Exodus 20:1–17
3. Exodus 20:16
4. Genesis 3:6
5. In a sense every lie to man is a lie before God. He hears and sees all and requires that we only tell the truth.
6. Were Ananias and Sapphira truly saved? Some say 'No. They act falsely: perhaps their claim to be saved is false.' Others say 'Yes, but they have failed badly.' Each view is based on truth. Truth takes over a saved person's life, but a saved person can sin. Someone saved cannot lose his or her salvation: John 10:27–30, Romans 8:31–39. The author has taken the second view.
7. 1 Corinthians 11: 27–32, on the Lord's supper. To take the supper unworthily caused sickness and even death. (See verse 30.)
8. Revelation 21:27 is abbreviated to read *anything that causes a lie* in order to emphasise how seriously God regards lies.
9. The word 'false' occurs in the NKJV 113 times. The list repays careful attention—and maybe some personal repentance.
10. 1 Thessalonians 4:9–12, 1 Timothy 5:16
11. Hebrews 9:27, Romans 1:18
12. 2 Peter 3:9 *patient* (NASB, NIV, ESV) is translated *longsuffering* in NKJV. See DayOne booklet, *How can God allow suffering?*
13. Proverbs 3:5–6, Romans 14:9

Chapter 12
1. One pastor asked me if angels could pick locks?! If so, they locked them up again, as Acts 5:23!
2. 1 John 1:7
3. Acts 4:18–20

Chapter 13
1. ESV translates *enraged*. NIV and NKJV translate *furious*.
2. Galatians 5:11
3. *Through Gates of Splendour* by Elizabeth Elliot (Jim's widow), published by Tyndale, grippingly tells the story.
4. Consider what Saul of Tarsus did before his conversion: Acts 22:3, Philippians 3:1–11
5. John 19:1–7
6. Matthew 10:21–25
7. 1 Peter 2:6–7: see NIV, NASB, and NKJV especially.

Chapter 14
1. Colossians 2:6
2. Hebrews 10:11–12, John 1:29, Hebrews 4:14–16
3. This includes the same Hellenistic Jews who now oppose Stephen when he is making sure their destitute widows are fed!
4. The first five books in the Old Testament, or Pentateuch, are the five books of God's law written by Moses. They are Genesis, Exodus, Leviticus, Numbers and Deuteronomy. As part of God's word, they are foundational to the Old Testament and to the New Testament, namely to the whole Bible.
5. Mark 14:55–59
6. Acts 4:12, Colossians 1:13–20

Chapter 15
1. Exodus 20:7, the fourth of the Ten Commandments, forbids blasphemy and says: 'You shall not take the name of the LORD your God in vain'. Stephen would not blaspheme God. He could not blaspheme Moses, who was a mere man and not God. In any case, Stephen never spoke against Moses, but treated his memory with grateful respect.
2. Acts 6:8–14 and Chapter 14 of this book, *A Problem Solved, the Word Spread, and Opposition Stirred*.
3. For example John 1, Hebrews 1, Philippians 2:5–11, Hebrews 4:15
4. John 2:18–22
5. Matthew 26:57–67, Acts 4:1–3,13–18, Acts 5:17–40
6. 2 Chronicles 6:1–11
7. Isaiah 66:1
8. John 8:58
9. Hebrews 6:17
10. John 6:35
11. Genesis 50:26
12. Hebrews 7:16, 22–28
13. Exodus 2:14
14. Hebrews 3:5–6
15. 2 Timothy 4:1,8, Acts 17:31, Revelation 17:14, Revelation 19:16
16. John 1:17
17. Ephesians 2:8–9, Acts 4:12, John 6:68, John 10:28
18. John 14:2–3, 1 Peter 1:3–5
19. Genesis 1:1, John 1:1–3, Hebrews 1:1–2
20. Revelation 5:12, Philippians 2:9–11
21. John 16:7–11,13–15
22. Romans 2:17–29
23. See Acts 9:5, Acts 26:14, Acts 22:20. *Goads* are pointed sticks to jab cattle to drive them forward—Saul's pangs of conscience at persecuting innocent Christians, and holding the coats of those who stone and kill Stephen must have been such *goads*.

Endnotes

Chapter 16
1. They were against Jesus—see Mark 14:43 to Mark 15:15. They are against the apostles—see Acts 4:1–31, Acts 5:17–42
2. Proverbs 29:1
3. 2 Corinthians 6:2, Hebrews 4:7
4. NKJV (cut to the heart), NIV (furious), ESV (enraged), NASB cut to the quick, The Amplified Bible *stung (cut) to the heart(cut to the heart)*.
5. Hebrews 12:2
6. They also taught that God does give living grace to live with!
7. 2 Corinthians 5:8, Philippians 1:23
8. Romans 14:12, Hebrews 4:13
9. John 8:3–11 highlights the predicament of Jews wishing to stone to death (in that case for adultery: in Stephen's case for blasphemy) in a land governed by Roman law. See how Jesus escaped the trap laid for him. (John 8:3–11 is best read in NKJV).
10. Acts 26:14
11. Acts 22:19–20
12. The Bible teaches there is one Triune God: God the Son, co-equal in the Trinity with God the Father and God the Holy Spirit, is also the eternal Son of God. He took flesh to come to earth as the son of Mary who conceived Him by the Holy Spirit. His title *Son of Man* not only emphasises that Jesus Christ on earth possessed both a divine and a sinless human nature. *Son of Man* is also a title the Bible gives to indicate Godhead. See, e.g. Luke 21:27, Luke 22:48, Luke 22:69, Luke 24:7, John 1:51, John 3:13–14
13. Luke 23:46
14. Luke 23:34
15. 2 Corinthians 5:8, Philippians 1:23

Chapter 17
1. Hebrews 4:16
2. Acts 6:4
3. Mark 10:27
4. Philippians 1:21, Philippians 3:7–8
5. Some say that Paul wrote thirteen letters. Others think that he wrote fourteen, including the book of Hebrews.
6. Matthew 25:21
7. Read Luke 10:29–37
8. Acts 8:35
9. Acts 4:12
10. Luke 15:7–10
11. Jonah 2:9

Chapter 18
1. Verse 13 says 'Simon himself *also* believed', thus clearly indicating that Philip's hearers had believed before being baptized.
2. Note it is in the *name* (singular) of the Triune God not in the 'names') . This underlines the oneness of Godhead in the Trinity of Father, Son and Holy Ghost. God is three in one and one in three in his Triune nature.
3. 1 Peter 2:5
4. Romans 8:9
5. James 2:19
6. Romans 10:13
7. Acts 1:8

Chapter 19
1. Because, like the King James Authorised Version, the NKJV is based on the *Textus Receptus* ('Received Text') it does not lack some of the verses that some other translations, with a more eclectic approach, leave out. Verse 37 here is missing from some translations and paraphrases, but the author is very happy to accept it as God's word and include it. All will agree that it is fully consistent with the gospel that is taught and revealed throughout the New Testament.
2. Proverbs 3:5–6
3. Acts 8:5
4. 1 Peter 2:24–25

Chapter 20
1. A goad is a spiked stick used for driving cattle. As the goad prods the cattle, so Paul's conscience prods him.
2. 2 Corinthians 3:14–15, 2 Corinthians 4:3–4
3. Ephesians 4:18
4. John 3:7, John 3:3—*born again* is used in all reliable translations.
5. John 3:3—'see the kingdom of God' here means to understand how to enter God's kingdom of forgiven sinners. John 3:5—to 'enter the kingdom of God' means by personal faith in Jesus Christ to come to know Him as your Saviour and as your King.
6. In his ever popular hymn *Amazing Grace*.
7. John 1:12
8. Acts 22:16
9. 1 Corinthians 12:13
10. Romans 8:9
11. Ephesians 5:18

Chapter 21
12. John 15:26, John 16:13
13. John 16:13–14

Endnotes

14. Acts 9:1
15. 2 Corinthians 11:32–33
16. Acts 8:4
17. Acts 4:36–37
18. Consider boldness in Acts by looking at: Acts 4:13, 4:29, 4:31, 9:29 13:46, 14:3, 18:26, 19:8
19. Remember that Hellenists were Jews from various places with strong Greek links. The martyr, Stephen, had dealings with them in his role as a deacon when he was responsible for feeding believing Hellenist widows. See Acts 6:1–6.
20. So suggests *The MacArthur Study Bible* in its comment on Acts 9:30, citing Acts 15:23 and Galatians 1:21.
21. Acts 1:8
22. Matthew 6:33
23. Philippians 1:6
24. *Amazing Acts—act one* precedes *Amazing Acts—act two* on chapters 9–18, and *Amazing Acts—act three* on chapters 19–28

A final word
1. See Appendix One in this book.
2. See Appendix Two in this book.
3. Gerard Chrispin, *The Bible Panorama* (DayOne, 2010).